Dedicated to my beautiful wife Melanie
without whose endless devotion,
support, and patience I could never find
the inspiration to set pen to paper.

INDEX

FORWARD

"Against stupidity, the Gods themselves contend in vain." Friedrich Schiller, 1786.

DATELINE MAY 2, 2012 – REUTERS: "Nearly fifteen percent of people worldwide believe the world will end in their lifetimes and ten percent think the Mayan Calendar could signify that it will happen in 2012".

The survey was taken in twenty different countries. In the United States the number was a staggering **twenty-two percent**! Let's extrapolate a bit.

Assuming there are 150,000,000 adults in the US, and ten percent of those presently believe in a Mayan "End of Time" doomsday, that means there are some fifteen million Americans (15,000,000!) who truly believe they may not be around on December 22nd!

And this number of souls was recorded well before the 12/21/12 debate really begins to heat up in the few months before this "pre-determined" event! I expect that the number of doomsday believers will triple if not more before November.

Incidentally, according to the study, relatively speaking, the French couldn't care less, and the Russians and Poles are terrified! And apparently the "under 35" crowd are across the board by far the most concerned. Time-wise they have the most to lose!

I know from my pre-publication reviews of this book that many of my readers are going to find this book to be quite scary and uncomfortable. Sadly we have all been subjected to so many predictions of impending catastrophe over the years that the remaining seventy-eight percent of Americans are totally deaf to any more such predictions.

Some cynics will say I simply wrote this book for the money. Believe it or not, writers have to eat too! But there is also a very sincere and heart-felt hope that my words will enlighten, entertain, and perhaps actually save those who choose to understand that life-threatening disasters can and do happen. Perhaps even on December 21, 2012. Perhaps not.

Many hold the attitude that: "Well, if something bad happens I'll deal with it then". Unfortunately when "then" comes around there is no way you CAN deal with it. The old Boy Scout motto: "Be Prepared", unfortunately falls on stone deaf ears.

Will December 21st bring about "something"? Anything? Can there possibly be any truth in any of this?

These are very valid questions, and **no one** can provide a positive answer, or even a well-educated guess. My hope for readers of this book is two-fold:

First, share with you, and make you aware of, the many different "doomsday scenarios" you will hear about in the days leading up to December 21st. Many of these scenarios are near-fantasy and far beyond la-la land! Many others are very real, and could actually happen at any future date, before, after, or actually on December 21st.

The clear and present danger of the "could actually happen" set of events will be totally whitewashed, vastly minimized by the government. You are never, ever, told the whole truth, "for your own good". You never will be. Talk about great material for a re-assuring Presidential campaign speech this summer!

I have a suggestion, though I doubt whether Congress would ever take it seriously. The Bald Eagle is our national symbol. It is a known scavenger, which matches quite well with the opinion of many world-wide of good old planet-scavenging USA.

Benjamin Franklin lobbied hard to make the Turkey our national symbol, which might have been even more appropriate to some. My suggestion? Make the **mushroom** our national symbol! It makes sense. We are kept in perpetual darkness and fed poop, the very key to mushroom propagation. Just a random thought.

My Second reason for writing this book is my strong belief that everyone who cares about his or her family should create some level of preparedness "just in case". If it isn't needed because of some event that happens coincidently or otherwise on 12/21 there is a very high likelihood that it will be needed some time in the near future.

I find it particularly amusing that all of the "experts" are scrambling to debunk any thought that December 21, 2012 has any validity whatsoever as a Mayan-predicted date of doom. On June 30th the BBC reported that a "new reading" of the hieroglyphics carved on a Mayan stone tablet shows "just the second reference to 2012" of 15,000 of such tablets. I cannot help but wonder what the "old reading" was!

This was actually the very first time I have ever seen it reported that the actual year 2012 was ever even mentioned as such in any Mayan text. I was under the impression that the 2012 date was deduced from complex calendar calculations by modern-day experts. Whatever. Perhaps someone should conduct a "new reading" of the other 13,999 tablets!

The source quoted goes on to conclude that: "There is no Mayan prophecy". Then he goes on to say that, yes, the Mayan's do in fact predict their God Bolon Yakte's return. Doesn't **that** qualify as a prophecy? It does to me. Making a distinction between "prediction" and "prophecy" seems rather lame. And it seems to me to not be too great a stretch to believe that this "predicted coming", should it actually happen, could have some sort of really bad consequences, apocalyptic, catastrophic or whatever.

Whether you choose to prepare for a one-week "problem" or a one-year problem, or even for a much longer global disaster, that's your call. But at least take the entire matter seriously or risk putting your life, and that of those you love, at some level of risk.

Knowledge is power. Learn all you can from this book. I am certain you will be glad you did.

Let us hope that we all wake up with smiles on our faces on December 22nd!

We don't have all that long to find out.

PART ONE

<u>PRELUDE TO APOCALYPSE</u>

"….a lie which is a half a truth is ever the darkest of lies." Alfred, Lord Tennyson.

"Human history becomes more and more a race between education and catastrophe." H. G. Wells.

On March 07, 2012, The Jet Propulsion Laboratory of the National Aeronautics and Space Agency (NASA) decided to post a video explaining away any possible physical influences that could bring about a cataclysmic event on December 21st! It was captioned: "12-21-2012 : Just Another Day". JPL? NASA? Really? Shall we guess whose idea this was? I believe it is called "Washington Whistling In The Dark".

Do most Americans believe that everything the government tells them is true? I think not. We are, in fact, treated as mushrooms. Seems to me that at least some real concern, perhaps official behind-the-scenes panic, resulted in creating this sort of "reassuring" video nine full months before the magic 12/21/12 date. The end of the Mayan long-count calendar is surely at least on the government's radar screen. Why do you suppose that might be?

The essence of this NASA video is discussed elsewhere in this book, along with my interpretations of some of the "expert" statements. I find it both interesting and a bit frightening that the denials began to appear so early in the year. And of course the

video never even hints at some of the more real possibilities. It just debunks the obviously absurd, and minimizes or totally ignores the very possible apocalypse scenarios.

I absolutely HATE coincidences. They seldom are. The very same weekend as the NASA video was shown, Accuweather aired an utterly idiotic denial video as well (I'll also discuss that one later). Needless to say there was virtually NO press coverage of either video.

Can you EVER believe press coverage of anything? I never cease to be amazed at the medias' bias shown time and time again. The biased coverage of politics is well documented, but the biased coverage of the 2012 Apocalypse strongly in favor of "it is not a problem" is becoming more evident with each new "revelation". Case in point:

On May 10th, Dateline MSN: "Never Mind The Apocalypse. Earliest Mayan Calendar Found". This story was reported on the same day on MSNBC's "Cosmic Log". There we find two different headlines offered for the same interesting article. "Maya Calendar Workshop Documents Time Beyond 2012" and "Maya Marked Time Beyond 2012". Read all three of these headlines and all of a sudden the "Mayan End Of Time" on December 21, 2012 has clearly been debunked. Just a load of llama poop. The headlines tell me so.

That is, if you only read the headline and do not read the actual article that followed! Apparently whoever wrote the headlines didn't bother to read the article at all. The article actually comes to the exact **OPPOSITE** conclusion from the headlines!

Apparently archeologists have recently discovered a buried six-foot-square room that contains 1,200 year old Maya paintings. It is located at the Xultun archeological site in Guatamala's

Peten Region. They have concluded it was a scribe's workplace. Paintings on the walls contained all manner of complex calendar calculations.

The article pointed out that David Stuart, an expert on Maya hieroglyphs, studying at Texas University in Austin, explained that the calendars were NOT indicating specific dates but are simply notations of elapsed time. Stuart specifically cautioned that the time notation **should NOT be read as specifying a date further in the future than December 21st!** This is the exact opposite of what the headlines stated! Astonishing, but rather typical, non-factual reporting.

The recent passing of Senate Bill 1867, titled the "National Defense Authorization Act" (NDAA) virtually revoked America's precious Bill of Rights. We are no longer totally free citizens. As I read and interpret it, this bill includes: secret arrests; indefinite detainment of American citizens without being charged with a crime, and with no possible trial (goodbye "due process") ; denial of an American citizen's right to legal representation; the free use of unlimited U. S, Military force against American civilians; the legitimate assassination of American citizens; and a host of other absolutely unbelievable and atrocious provisions.

Is it possible that these provisions were considered necessary for national security in light of events that some predict will occur later in 2012? President Obama signed the bill into law on December 31, 2011, NEW YEAR'S EVE! Talk about doing something "under the radar"! Press coverage was zilch, and even had it been thoroughly reported, who does anything other than recover their equilibrium on New Year's Day? This bill simply passed virtually unnoticed, even though it was the single most important piece of legislation in American history!

It has been reported that any President acting alone now has virtually unlimited powers to: Direct any American business to do virtually anything needed "in the National Interest"; To compel any American citizen to work for the government at zero wage if called to duty; To confiscate any of your property in light of the "The National Interest".

Has any American citizen actually read or studied this unbelievable bill? I have, and for the first time in my 75 years as a free country-loving American and proud Army veteran I am truly frightened of my government. This is no longer the country in which I have lived and worked and paid taxes for three-quarters of a century. Are we becoming Stalinist Russia, Maoist China, Castro's Cuba, Chavez' Venezuela or worse. Or are we in some hard to fathom way being prepared for a coming apocalypse later in 2012?

Sadly no one seems to give a damn, certainly not the press, and apparently not candidate Mitt Romney, who hasn't uttered a word in defense of our Bill of Rights. Why is he not screaming for repeal? Could this not be turned into a legitimate campaign issue? Or is he privy to information not being divulged to the American public? Is this a prelude to the Mayan 2012 End Time issue? We will soon know.

As sad as SB1867 appears to be, even scarier is the "Law Of The Sea" treaty, which is incredibly being actively debated and considered in Congress. It is reported to have a very real chance of being ratified. This innocent-sounding treaty would simply do away with virtually all United States sovereignty! You would pay untold international taxes, and be governed by unimaginable international laws. Goodbye Constitution. Goodbye United States. "One-World Government" proponents victorious at last. Wouldn't December 21st be a great symbolic day to commit the United States to this sovereignty-ending nightmare by signing the treaty? Or is world unity somehow in our best interest after an apocalyptic event.

Ever read: They Thought They Were Free by Milton Mayer? If not, you should. It is about the citizens of Germany as Hitler slowly boiled them alive like a green fresh lobster. The poor little bugger begins to feel a bit uncomfortably warm, then rather soon it's red and dead! I love a good lobster dinner, but I hate the thought of being one. Unfortunately, I'm beginning to feel very lobsterish.

Just exactly what are we being set up for? Is this all for our own protection? Is this America for and by the people? Certainly not the Great Nation into which I was born. Can "panic", real or imagined, or even "created", over the December 21st date, become a reason to declare a "National Emergency"? Is the government anticipating this? Is there some connection at all here with December 21, 2012? We will see. Time will tell. I hope not. Anything seems possible these days.

Conspiracy theorists will have a field day with all of this. I consider myself to simply be an interested but concerned outside observer. I may be naïve but I actually believe our government does make its best effort to protect its citizens, and all of this scary stuff may just be part of a grand plan for our survival.

Just how does one define "National Emergency" anyway?" It depends on who you ask. Can it be an "Economic Emergency"? We sure aren't far from THAT sorry reality as financial matters are presently unfolding. Can it be an "Impending Threat" emergency, imagined or real? Can it be a "Real" emergency such as a nuclear attack or cyber-attack? Or an actual Mayan calendar related emergency, coincidental or prophesized?

The biggest disaster in US history may occur on November 6th. But that's another issue, and depends on your political viewpoint. Regardless of the outcome, roughly half of the country will not be at all happy about it. If we can only convince enough voters that "FREEDOM" and "CONSTITUTION" and "BILL OF RIGHTS" are good words, there is hope. If the Apocalypse comes on 12/21 those ensuing forty-four days between 11/6 and 12/21 won't make a hill of beans difference anyway!

I am a writer, and a scientist. I published my first book in 1970, and have written eleven others and countless articles. From 1997 through 1998 I did exhaustive research on the Y2K "Millennium Bug", and published "Whitewash Y2K". There were many very credible, intelligent and dedicated people, including many high-level government officials and politicians, predicting varying degrees of chaos, and taking Y2K very seriously. As a graduate scientist myself I was very curious as to whether there might be anything to all of the Y2K buzz.

President Clinton actually appointed his wife Hillary to be in charge of studying and remediating all possible Y2K scenarios, putting her in charge of the "Millennium Project". He seemed inordinately calm about the entire matter, barely mentioning it in his 1999 State of the Union message.

Whitewash Y2K? The government was quite obviously taking Y2K very seriously, as well they should have. Ms. Clinton certainly was taking it seriously.

I wonder whether Ms. Obama will be put in charge soon of quelling our collective 12/21 fears? Perhaps we should all just go eat a nice healthy banana, skip the Botswanian fat-cakes, and just ignore it all! Food for thought.

It was clear to many before the new millennium was to dawn that we had the technological ability to fix the tens of thousands of nasty things that could possibly go wrong with the Y2K transition. The essence of the problem was our extreme reliance on computer electronics to run virtually everything upon which we relay for our daily existence. To this day cyber space is our greatest weakness as a nation, as I'll discuss in much detail later.

When it became a recognized fact that computers worldwide had no idea (read: "proper code") of how to handle the midnight 12/31/99 flip to a new century, concern started to build.   Permanent collapse of entire power grids, putting us all back into the stone age, was not beyond imagining. In fact, many experts thought it was a certainty. It was a certainty, had we done nothing to squash the bug.

Modern techno-civilization had become very complacent. The Y2K problem was commented upon in the early '90s. With procrastination apparently being a universal human trait, everyone "put off till tomorrow" any remediation efforts. But as years of "tomorrows" passed, and as the new century neared, it became a very real worldwide concern.

In fact, it became a bit of a worldwide panic.

The time needed to rewrite billions of lines of computer code might have, many believed, turned out to be greater than the time that was available to actually fix all of those 1-0-1-0-1-0s and prevent a serious global catastrophe.

For my book Whitewash Y2K I interviewed power plant managers, and bank presidents, and chemical plant managers and politicians. All seemed scared out of their wits. As a graduate engineer, so was I. This was not something to leave for the last possible minute. Y2K had serious implications, and the public was not being told the whole truth and nothing but the truth. It was indeed "Whitewash Y2K" big time. I anticipate a similar "Whitewash 12/21" this time, and for the same reasons.

Subsequently, in early 1999 I wrote and published the above mentioned book. My first book signing was at Borders Books in Tucson. I even had my own weekly local cable TV call-in program! My basic premise was that we were not being told just how bad things could become (and believe me we were **not** being told). I advised anyone who would listen: "Don't panic, but be aware of what could happen, and make at least some preparations accordingly for the sake of your family."

There were many other books in print at the time that were far more pessimistic in their Y2K message than I was in mine. I was sufficiently apprehensive to consider a move to Hawaii, which for many reasons at that time seemed to be the safest place on earth to be if the Y2K doomsayers actually turned out to be correct. Eventually, I actually moved my family to the Big Island. We only recently returned.

On December 31,1999 I anxiously awaited word from New Zealand that nothing unusual had happened at midnight NZ time. The Y2K Millennium Bug could have begun there with an inexorable trek from time zone to time zone shutting down the world. When the word came from down under that nothing whatsoever happened by 12:01AM , I was quite sure the rest of the world could sleep well that night. I surely did.

As the first day of the new century progressed nothing of note happened anywhere on earth, and everyone who said Y2K was a hoax felt fully vindicated and laughed heartily at all the rest of us who showed real concern. But was their smugness justified?

Was Y2K a hoax? Far from it. It was reported later in 2000 that worldwide two to three TRILLION dollars had been spent on remediation to prevent a very real worldwide disaster. Some major corporations individually spent billions. We had the money and the capability to avert the impending disaster, and proved beyond a doubt that with enough money thrown at a problem it can be solved. Hurrah for our side! Money, Technology, and Capitalism triumph once again! We rule! Sort of.

Spending this massive amount of money was absolutely necessary. But economically it was money flushed down the crapper. It bought no increase in productivity whatsoever. It bought nothing tangible. It bought one important thing: disaster aversion. And what actually resulted in the financial markets after Y2K from this unprecedented massive non-productive expenditure? How was a few trillion dollars lost forever simply swept under the rug? If there were any studies done on this subject I have never found one. Apparently no one cares to remember.

Y2K was a very real potential crisis out of which we collectively bought ourselves. We weren't sent back to the caves. We could enjoy our lattes and continue our lives uninterrupted by something as far-fetched and laughable as losing the entire power grid.

I have never seen this global financial disaster analyzed after-the-fact anywhere. Is it just coincidence that the entire world economy has spent the last decade or so, since spending all that money on Y2K, in a steady downward spiral? Or was the bite of the Millennium Bug closer to fatal than anyone dared admit, especially financially? Just more food for thought.

Over the years there have been many other "crises" predicted to occur that always seem to amount to nothing. Various space rocks appear out of nowhere and miss earth. The sun burps incredible amounts of energy at us periodically, and little of consequence ever happens. The fact is, the public has become so used to these "potential" disasters amounting to nothing that most people are totally biased in their belief that nothing really bad can ever happen to them, or to the planet.

Of course, if you happened to be a dinosaur when a rather large space rock hit Yucatan 10,000 years ago you might not agree. Or say you lived in Pompeii or Herculaneum in 233 AD you might not be quite so confident when you went to sleep the night before the "big surprise". You were simply buried in volcanic ash, and never saw the light of another day. How about the folks around Krakatoa, near Java, in 1115 AD? Or Santorini some four thousand years ago? Very big ouch! Occasionally really bad stuff actually happens without notice.

In 1907 the entire city of Chicago went up in smoke. In 1996 without warning a few hikers were vaporized while camping out on a "dormant" Mount St. Helens in Washington State. The recent earthquakes and tsunamis in Indonesia and in Japan weren't exactly predicted. At least that kid in Japan got his soccer ball back after it took a year to float over to Alaska, along with a zillion-ton concrete pier! Flotsam and jetsam redefined.

In my lifetime thousands of harmless folks in Hiroshima and Nagasaki were vaporized rather unexpectedly at the behest of President Truman. None of these events were predicted in advance by those directly affected. There was no prior warning. There was no speculation beforehand. There was no specific date of prediction by the victims. Kablooie! Game over.

So now this time around we have a real predicted calendar date, December 21, 2012, just a few months away. Most, though far from all, in the public are treating this as some sort of joke or ignoring it completely. Apparently about one in four is not. Our government will make it into a joke whether or not they think it actually is one. There are many intelligent people who are taking this end-of-time apocalypse scenario very seriously. Most people, because of previous Y2K-like "non-crises", will simply ignore it.

Jay Leno and David Letterman, along with the lesser of the late night TV comedians, will have months of ready-made joke material over "the end of the world". MENSA, the high IQ society (to which I am one of the first US members, please don't ask me why) held a big "Pre-Apocalypse" party in Reno over the 4th of July weekend. Thousands attended. I was not one of them!

Personally, however, I am one who will be very relieved to awaken on December 22nd and find that absolutely nothing happened, just as was my reality on the morning of January 1, 2000.

I have studied this Mayan calendar "event" for almost twenty-one years. I think I have read just about everything ever written on it. I have dozens of "2012" books in my eclectic 10,000+ volume personal library. Serious writers and scholars have focused on 2012 for decades. There are many interpretations, many theories, and many different conclusions relating to the Mayan calendars. There is also a great deal of misinformation out there. I hope in this book that I can offer you some clarification, and can present some food for rational thought and positive action.

Whether it be on December 21st or some other date before or after, there are many potential catastrophes that can occur, some absolutely certain (e.g., our sun will eventually fry us totally, albeit in a few billion years), some very probable, many others quite remote.

So just what could actually happen? Is this just another cruel joke good for lots of fun press and cartoons and the creation thereby of many truly frightened people? I have given this a lot of thought, and looked at all of the things that could possibly go wrong. The fact is, most of these could go wrong tomorrow, on 12/21, or in 2028, or 3054, or never! Deep doo doo happens, it's just a question of timing and preparation or lack thereof.

Why might any one of these disasters actually happen on a predicted date, this coming December 21st? Well, I believe there are a few fundamental reasons why we might not all be around on December 22nd.

If you are deeply religious, consider an understandably vengeful God with an ironic sense of humor. Or what about a maniacal radical with an equally ironic sense of history? How about a natural or man-made catastrophe with an accidental sense of timing? Or perhaps a self-fulfilling prophecy?

I don't know what percentage of our population believes that the government tells us everything that is going on that could affect our lives. I doubt if many believe it. I surely do not. Is President Obama himself actually told everything by the cognoscenti around him? I rather doubt it. Ignorance is bliss. Why trouble the President with something as trivial as the end of the world as we know it? Bearers of bad news have historically been killed! No good deed goes unpunished.

There are occasional events that are mentioned casually by the media and then forgotten. Whether these events are truly trivial, or potentially cataclysmic does not seem to matter. The public just does not seem to give a damn one way or the other. We would rather read about the love affairs or transgressions of some idiot celebrity, or who gets custody of Suri, or about some sicko who shoots some poor soul who was in the wrong place at the wrong time, than read about a very real potential life-altering event. Again, ignorance is bliss.

By whatever means, blame the National Education Association, or banal television shows, or Facebook, iPods and X-Boxes or whatever, it seems to me that our collective brains have been turned to mush over the past few decades. We just don't take anything important seriously. We are in constant denial. We just do not seem to have the capacity to care.

Please read on, and decide whether preparing for an Apocalypse on December 21st, or some future disaster, is worth your time and effort . Survive or perish. Knowledge is power.

It's entirely your call.

PART TWO

THE MAYAN CALENDARS

"Only the creation of sufficient "incidents" yet remains; and you see the first of these already taking place, according to plan ....a plan that was never laid before the American people for their approval." Charles A. Lindbergh, 1941, referencing America's entry into WWII.

Once a year, every year for as long as I can remember, I trot on down to my local Walmart super-store and buy the next edition of the yearly 12-month wall calendar. Sometime shorty after January 1st (usually around the 10th!) I toss out the old one and hang up the new one. My one calendar has ended, my new one has begun, all fresh and shiny and full of promise for the wonderful year ahead.

My last calendar, as is the case with my newly bought one, covered a single measly year, a clearly capitalistic plot to kill more trees and sell more paper calendars! (The Mayans were obviously environmentalists. Stone tablets last forever!) One calendar ends, with no big deal except for the annual New Year's Eve hangover. Another calendar takes its place of honor on my wall. Thus it has been for over half a century.

But what if my calendar, instead of a countdown to a hangover, counted down to the End Of Time itself? And what if that calendar had been around for many hundreds of years, was not replaced every year, and this just happened to be the year when I should be able to, but could not, go buy a new one?

On December 21, 2012 (or maybe the 22nd or 23rd depending on who you choose to believe) the incredible super-complex ancient Mayan Calendar registers its final date, its "end of the cycle", the end of the "Age Of The Jaguar". As with a car's odometer resetting from 129999 to 130000 within the blink of an eye, the Mayan Calendar in theory resets to 13.0.0.0.0 in a heartbeat at midnight December 20, 2012 (I assume that's Greenwich Mean Time!) .

One might well say: "So what? Every calendar resets". But not every calendar comes with a wide range of apocalyptic interpretations. Here is where we get into the nitty-gritty of this whole 12-21-12 discussion. How and why is this coming December 21st **THE** day.   Basically, it comes down to a combination of many things, some objective, some subjective, some clearly a joke or scam, some really possible.

There are just two key issues. First, what exactly, if anything, is actually prophesized by the Mayans? If something is actually forecast to happen, how do we know the meaning and intention of that "something"? Second, how did we arrive at December 21, 2012 as the exact day the Mayan calendar ends or resets?

These are all great questions, the answers to which will be used as excuses on the "day after" IF nothing actually happens. "We misinterpreted the predictions"; or, "We mis-translated the hieroglyphics"; or "Our calculations were a bit off. Maybe its 12-21-**13**." Whatever.

I am, purely by accident, a highly skilled "numbers person". As an engineer I was trained in "higher math", absolutely useless esoterica such as Fourier Series and Laplace Transformations, simultaneous differential equations, and much higher calculus.

Absolutely **none** of this was later of any practical value in any job position I ever held.   It makes me wonder to this day why in hell I ever agonized through engineering school in the first place! But that's another story. (I'm contemplating writing: *Engineering School Sucks!*).

No, I'm talking here about simple arithmetic. In the third grade in Public School #139 in Brooklyn, New York I had a really wonderful teacher named Miss Petrella. I recall she was very old (or so it seemed to a third-grader; she was probably forty) and only owned ugly baggy black dresses! She would assign "punish papers" to anyone misbehaving. Her "punish papers", and my record-breaking accumulation of them, gave me a huge mental edge in arithmetic calculations throughout my later life.

Each "assignment", which had to be completed in class while sitting in the "Dunce's Corner" wearing a peaked hat (I believe that was back in 1947 - so much for Universal Self Esteem!)   was an arithmetic calculation, basically a "times-table".

At the top of the paper was a number, such as "8". From there you had to write out the sums of   "8 x 1" all the way up to "8 x 100". By the time I got to fourth grade, "8 x 56 = 448" or "6 x 37 = 222" were burned into my brain! Throughout my entire working career I found this facility for plain old arithmetic extremely valuable. Thanks Miss Petrella! I'll never forget you.

I was fascinated by Patrick Geryl's 2005 book: "The World Cataclysm In 2012 – The Maya Countdown To The End Of

Our World." Throughout the book are sixty or so pages of rather intricate arithmetic calculations. I enjoyed following them. Are these calculations all truly amazing relationships conclusively proving the coming 2012 Apocalypse on 12/21, or just sets of amazing coincidences. Perhaps a proof of Armageddon, perhaps not, but very fascinating nevertheless. If you enjoy arithmetic, check it out. Have a bottle of aspirin handy.

But I was left with a vague suspicion. If I were to take the median weight of a BigMac, divide it by the number of times my dog poops in a week, factor in the local mean temperature in July and multiply it all by the speed of sound squared I'd come up with some quantity that could be shown to relate to some other equally obscure quantity proving whatever it was I started out to prove in the first place! Numbers can prove everything, or nothing. If Geryl's math is right, it is in fact doomsday! We will know soon. I hope he is wrong. One never knows.

The home territory of the Maya was an area that corresponds to present-day southern Mexico, Guatemala, Belize, Honduras and part of El Salvador. The Mayan civilization flourished for about seven hundred years, between 200AD and 900AD. (That's about three times as long as the USA has managed to survive!). It reached its height around 800AD. Only 200 years thereafter it had collapsed entirely. Are **we** overdue?

Some indigenous Mayan people continue to occupy the same geographic area to this day. Their civilization was preceded by the Olmecs, and followed by the Toltecs and then the Aztecs. Each of these cultures held the belief that the earth had been created and reborn several times before, but they did not conceive or adapt the actual Mayan calendar predicting a specific "end date" as is now calculated to be this coming December 21st.

The present day Hopi Indians of Northern Arizona carry on the traditions of their ancestors. They believe that we humans have occupied three previous worlds before migrating to this present fourth world. Further, they believe we managed to screw all of them up and expect us to once again suffer annihilation as our well-deserved punishment. 2012 Kablooie?

Credit goes to Walt Kelly and Pogo for "2012 Kablooie!" I recall a cartoon where Pogo was asked for his assessment and definition of the coming Y2K event and he replied: "Y2K Kablooie!".

The only other Pogo cartoon I can actually recall is the one where he and his pal are sitting on a stump in their once-pristine swamp choked with human-garbage and he utters: "Yep, we have met the enemy and he is us!". Walk Kelly was a genius.

The Mayan calendars are actually quite amazing and because of their complexity are subject to **a wide range of subjective interpretations**. One difficulty comes in relating the calendars to a specific "Beginning Time" and an "End Time", and relating it all to our present-day calendar. Coming up with December 21, 2012 requires an elegant calculation, and seems to now be the universally accepted date (though some believe that December 23rd two days later, is a more accurate date.)

Whether the calculations are off by a day or two or even a year or two is actually the subject of much on-going debate, though it certainly doesn't matter if we're all eventually fried anyway!

If you put any credibility at all in the many prophesies of Nostradamus, in his Quatrain 1:16 he reportedly pinpoints October 2012 as the time when a massive electromagnetic pulse arrives on earth. 2012 Kablooie? That's rather close to predicting December 21st as the key date. Many believe his prophesies, when "properly" interpreted, are always spot on. Others consider him to be a misguided charlatan. The jury is still out.

In any event, the 2012 year keeps popping up in culture after culture, calculation after calculation, scholarly dissertation after scholarly dissertation. It has been debated for decades.

When we refer to the "Mayan Calendar" in the context of the "coming Apocalypse" we are speaking of but one out of twenty or so known different Mayan calendars. The Maya had a strange fascination with celestial matters and especially with calendars.

These could well be, as is often explained, tied in with keeping track of agricultural seasons. One calendar, the tzolk'in, is 260 days long and apparently relates directly to human gestation.

Certain of their calendars are said to allow precise calculations back as far as four-hundred-million years in the past! Why that is puzzles archeologists. Some calendars apparently can be interpreted as allowing calculations far **beyond** 2012, although this line of reasoning precludes 12/21/12 as being the beginning or end of anything. This is all quite fascinating, but why the heck did the Mayans bother? They apparently had a good reason.

The calendars themselves, engraved stone slabs, were excavated by archeologists over time some years ago. Some related artifacts are found during the continuing current excavations. There could be many other calendars and texts as yet undiscovered. Whether certain tablets were, in the past, part of an interlocking computational gear system when placed edge to edge is subject to conjecture and disagreement.

Not all of the calendars have been interpreted by "reading" hieroglyphics on stone slabs. Some calendars have been found painted on the interior walls of various excavated chambers.

Let me try to put this entire calendar thing in as simplified a form as I can. My explanation might not satisfy an expert Mayan archeologist or linguist, which I certainly am not, but it is the best I can offer you. These Mayan people were either quite amazingly brilliant, or were somehow given knowledge **far beyond** their developmental state. **It is a fact that these folks never even invented the wheel!**

The Maya looked at "time" as the interconnection of various spiritual cycles. These were religiously zealous people who had a patron saint for every single day of the year! I wonder if anyone could name all 365 in correct order!

Most of their calendars covered short time frames. The shortest Mayan calendar is the Ixim Tun, a 130 day cycle that probably was agriculture based.

One of the calendars, the Tiku Tun, covers 1,144 years in a 468 year (9 x 52) "Circle Of Light" and a "676 year " (13 x 52) Circle Of Darkness. The significance of these is unclear. None of these seem to play any direct role in the 2012 calculation and "end time". In fact, five of the twenty known calendars apparently have no cyclic significance whatsoever.

The most important calendars apparently are the aforementioned tzolk'in which covered 260 days, and the Haab' which covered 365 days, earth's basic solar year. The Haab' is the only Mayan calendar that bears any resemblance to our modern calendar, minus accommodation for the leap years.

The Mayans combined these two calendars to create what is known as the "Calendar Round". This calendar covered 52 years, 18,980 days in total, which approximated a single human generation at that time. Within this 52 year calendar were cycles of thirteen days (trecena) and twenty days (veintena). The numbers 13 and 20 were the basis of all of their calendar calculations in one way or the other.

The longest calendar is the Ox Lajuj Baktun, which is based on the Calendar Round's 360 day periods, called "tuns".

The key "long-count" calendar, often simply referred to as the "Baktun" is broken down as follows:

20 k'ins   = 1 winal = 20 days

18 winals = 1 tun   = 360 days

20 tuns   = 1 k'atun = 7,200 days

20 k'tauns = 1 bak'tun = 144,000 days

Here is where it gets really interesting: 13 bak'tuns (1,872,000 days, about 5,125 years) = 1 Great Cycle, known as a "Sun". Five Suns (65 bak'tuns) constitute a Grand Cycle. This happens to be 25,627 years, which is correctly one full cycle of the precession of the equinoxes! How in hell did the ancient

Mayans know this? A **really** good guess? Coincidence? Extraterrestrial intervention? Whatever. Your guess is as good as mine. It is hard to believe it is a coincidence.

The ancient Hindus, with no possible connection to the Maya, came up with a very similar number of years in the 25,000 range. As I said earlier, I HATE coincidences, because sometimes they are not coincidences at all.

The actual calendar dates are deduced through hieroglyphic interpretations by trained archeologists. They are helped by the testimony of actual living Mayan "Daykeepers", folks historically entrusted with calendar interpretation. The "long-count" calendar will soon register 13.0.0.0.0. The question is, does this mark the end of one "Great Cycle" and the beginning of another? Or does it mark "The End Of Time"? Or something else?

Correlating this Mayan calendar with our upcoming calendar date of December 21, 2012 is the subject of a massive amount of calculation and interpretation. This one single date is now generally accepted as **THE** date. There are many entire books longer than this book listed in the Bibliography that are written entirely to explain the complex derivation of this single date.

An aside: Could this 13.0.0.0.0 be the origin of "unlucky 13" and "Friday the 13th" as bad omens? Just wondering.

Here's the math: The Mayan Long Count Calendar starts at 0.0.0.0.0. Each of these 0s goes from 0 – 19, known as calculating in "base 20", the root of the system. Thus the first day of the Long Count is 0.0.0.0.1, the nineteenth day 0.0.0.0.19. On the twentieth day it goes to: 0.0.0.1.0. In about a year we have: 0.0.1.0.0; in about twenty years: 0.1.0.0.0. In four-hundred years we have 1.0.0.0.0.

The other root of their numerical system is the number "13". The calendar ends on 13.0.0.0.0, which represents 5,126 years from 0.0.0.0.0. Working backwards and forwards it is calculated that 0.0.0.0.0 corresponds to August 11, 3114 BC, and the end comes on December 21, 2012!

The major disagreement among those who study the Mayan calendars is whether the Maya intended for a new calendar to actually begin on December 22, 2012, or whether they had some "prior knowledge" that there was no need for a calendar beyond that date!

It is believed by many that the Mayans are predicting the beginning of an "Age Of Enlightenment", which obviously can be interpreted as just about anything, depending upon one's viewpoint! What enlightens one person might well curse another!

The entire "Coming Apocalypse" issue is based on whether the "End Of" something as innocent as a calendar actually means the "end" of anything physical at all. If nothing else, could the date simply become a "self-fulfilling prophesy"? More about that later.

One question obviously begs an answer: How could (and why **would**) the ancient Maya, who as I mentioned above never even conceived the wheel, invent such an immensely complicated computational device?   And this amazing "calendar" for want of a better word, was designed to predict unique events that would happen hundreds of years in the future, and look far back into the past! That is pretty mind boggling.

The Mayan archeo-specialists who have deciphered all of this have come to the conclusion through interesting complex computations that the "Start Date" of the Mayan "long-count" calendar is August 11, 3114 BC. This is some 3,000 years before the Maya's time! The Maya called this beginning point "4ahau 8cumhu". The end-date is 1,872,000 days later (exactly 13 bak'tuns) on December 21, 2012.! Clearly the key to the 12/21/12 date is the calculation of the starting date.

Sven Gronemeyer of LaTrobe University in Australia, an expert in Mayan hieroglyphic interpretations, offered his insight recently at a meeting in Palenque in southern Mexico. The key calendar text, he noted, was carved some 1,300 years ago. It was found years ago at the archeological dig site of Tortuguero in Mexico's Tabasco State.

The tablet was cracked when found, and much of the tablet was almost illegible. He believed the tablet to have been created during the reign of the Mayan ruler Bahlam Ajaw. It essentially predicted the return of the principal Mayan God Bolon Yokte.

This God is predicted to return along with associated other lesser Gods at the end of the 13th period of 400 years. These "other Gods" are believed by some to be the extraterrestrials who imparted the calendars to the Maya in the first place, and who promised to return at some "end time", accepted by most Mayan experts as December 21, 2012.

On this upcoming date in December the Mayans correctly predicted that the winter solstice sun would align perfectly with what they called "The Mouth of the Crocodile". The latter is often described in books as a "dark rift" in our galaxy. Not exactly.

It is in fact the almost "star free" space between two Milky Way galactic spiral arms as viewed from earth's perspective. This alignment fact holds great significance for many 2012 Apocalypse theorists. Frankly, this relationship being of any possible significance seems to be quite a stretch of reason and logic, but who am I to say? In any event, the Mayans somehow got the timing right. Another amazing coincidence?

The Mayans believed that extraterrestrials launched the present age of man. This is what they carved in stone. They believed that 13 bak'tuns later (the above 1,872,000 days)   the sun would be positioned as it actually is every 25,627 years or so? Just a good guess? I don't think so. Someone **mus**t have told them so. Why? Because it is precisely correct!

Have any Mayan calendars ever been shown to correctly predict a future event? It is reported that they accurately predicted the date of the arrival of the European Conquistadors hundreds of years prior to that actual event. Apparently knowing what is coming and doing something positive about it are mutually exclusive! The Spaniards kicked their butts.

It is even more curious, beyond coincidence as I view things, that this same 3114 BC Mayan "Starting Date" coincides rather closely with the building of Stonehenge, the beginning of dynastic Egypt, the development of script in Mesopotamia, and the first cultivation of corn in the Americas!. These were cultural revolutions of global proportions. Is this all pure coincidence? Or was it simultaneous extraterrestrial intervention because they just happened to be hanging around earth at the time? Personally, I believe Eric von Daneken got it right (see Bibliography).

The Mayan Holy Book is called the Popal Vuh. It contains the entire Maya creation story, beginning to end. English translations are available. I have read one. I have no idea how accurate the translation was, but it is a fascinating read.

The understanding that I came away with is that the "First Father" and "First Mother" will return on 13.0.0.0.0 (read: December 21, 2012) to bring about a **new** world age. Whether these two God-figures are benevolent or hostile isn't clear. Nor is the definition of "new" any clearer than Clinton's definition of "is" was. Ain't semantics wonderful?

The Popol Vuh explains that the various forms of life on earth are the unsuccessful attempts by their Gods, who showed a predilection for biological experimentation , to make "We The People". Early tries were far off the mark, creating the lower animals. Not even close. The penultimate attempt, a near miss, made monkeys and apes. Getting lots closer. Apparently making humans wasn't exactly considered a bulls-eye either!

Mayans believe that we humans are but a small part of their Gods' plans to carry out some mission in this tiny corner of the universe. The life of planet earth depends on us and how we care for it. (Was Rachael Carlson a re-born Mayan? Go figure.)

The Mayans imply that the world is far from finished in its creation and perfection. We haven't done a particularly good job as stewards of the planet (you think?). We must learn to play out our correct role of preserving earth. Try once again? Start over? 2012 Kablooie?

There is, as I read it, no actual prediction of an Apocalypse per se in the Popol Vuh, just a potential ass-kicking wakeup call to put us on the straight and narrow as stewards of this tiny rock on which we all reside. Just how bad an ass-kicking is the point of all of this speculation about December 21st.

The Poplo Vuh surely isn't as frightening as the Christian "Book of Revelations" and its predicted "Tribulation". If the latter doesn't scare the crap out of you with a graphic depiction of the results on the human body of a nuclear war I don't know what could! It just doesn't provide a specific date. Damned inconvenient.

Isn't it ironic that virtually every religion has a specific beginning and a specific end in their Holy of Holies? Christians, Muslims and Jews await a "coming". Buddhists await the appearance of the "Perfect Buddah", Metteyya.

The early Iranian, Zoroaster, taught about a final day of judgment that must surely occur. To survive, all living souls would then have to walk through a river of molten metal. You can guess who makes it to the other side. Certainly not Ginsburg!

It is **very** important to note that many other cultures worldwide believe we are getting close to a final day of judgment. This includes the Maori in New Zealand, and many African tribes. Some of the Egyptian prophecies I have read about follow rather closely the Mayan "End Of Time" scenario. Even the biblical "Number Of The Beast", 666, has been shown by some to have a direct mathematical bearing on the coming December Apocalypse.

Also, Tibetan and Vedic beliefs point to the year **2012** as the end of a long cycle and a "new beginning". They could not possibly have communicated with the Maya.   Coincidence?   I HATE coincidences, for aforementioned reasons.

There is an almost universal religious belief that some messianic character will appear some day in the future. Does this all hark back to a warning made by extraterrestrials to our ancient ancestors thousands of years ago that on an appointed day the "Great Spirit of Creation" will bring about "Judgment Day"? December 21, 2012?   2012 Kablooie? We will soon know.

There are many Mayan descendants alive today. Within their "Men's Community of Elders" they even have "calendar keepers" known as the "Daykeepers". The most recent name of such a person I have found in print is that of Gerardo Kaanek' who I believe is still alive. (There was also within the recent past decade a famous "Head Daykeeper" named Hunbatz Men, who lectured extensively.) They have stated that 13.0.0.0.0 ends one Great Cycle **and begins a new Great Cycle.**

When something comes to an end we humans have the capacity for imagining the worst case scenario, some sort of horrible death. This entire December 21st discussion centers around just exactly what the **beginning** of that new Great Cycle might portend. Purge everything and start anew, along the lines of Noah's Great Flood? A religious miracle, a "coming"? 2012 Kablooie?

Perhaps even the Maya haven't got the remotest clue, and will have their collective eyes glued to the heavens on December 21, 2012 to learn their destiny.....and ours.

PART THREE

<u>CLASSIC RELIGION AND "THE COMING"</u>

"Nothing is easier than self-deceit. For what each man wishes, that he also believes to be true." Demosthenes.

Let's turn our attention to religion. I never cease to be fascinated by the "my God is the one real God and much better than your God" feelings that seem to have been firmly established in the minds of all but Atheists. The latter choose to have no God. Perhaps this is a simpler and not an altogether bad concept.

Since sentient proto-humans first learned to beat each other to death with sticks and bones (remember that great intro to "*2001 – A Space Odyssey*"?) religion has been responsible for more human death and suffering than anything else imaginable.

Religion has been at the heart and soul of man's deepest troubles for all of history. Could these troubles, which are no less real today than in the past 10,000 years or so, somehow lead us all to the fulfillment of end-time prophecies?

What has religion got to do with 12/21/12? Perhaps nothing. Maybe everything. I am not a student of religion. In short, below is my probably-inaccurate understanding of three of the world's religions that all focus on Jesus in one way or another. My apologies to anyone who is offended by my poor understanding of their religion. I mean to offend no one. Please forgive my ignorance.

There are seven billion plus (7,000,000,000+) people on earth.

About one-third profess to some form of Christianity, and one-fifth profess to some form of Islam. Judaism is represented by a remarkably small number of people, somewhere well under one percent. All three, however, "believe in Jesus", and in a "re-appearance", in one way or other.

Hindus, Buddhists, and traditional Chinese religions combined make up around another one-fifth of earth's people, but as far as I understand Jesus existence is not a part of their beliefs. They do not follow the God of Abraham. And the fifteen percent or so who identify themselves as Atheists I guess couldn't care less.

However, virtually every religion speaks of an "end time", as well as a "beginning time", much as do the Mayans. "The End Time". "The End Of The World". "The End Of Life As We Know It". These prophesies have been made so many times in the past by everyone from pure charlatans to true-believing zealots that today they mostly fall on deaf ears.

We've heard often that "the world will end tomorrow", and then it doesn't. Ever. At least not yet. To some extent we are all influenced by the religion of our ancestors.

The biblical Book of Revelations seems to sum it all up. As I understand it there had to be seven "seals" broken, and six are said to have already been broken. The seventh and final seal is about to be broken. When it is, the prophesized Apocalypse will be upon us. ".....for the time is at hand" (Rev. 1:3). That entire Book is written in the context of end-time events, leading to the "Day of the Lord's Wrath". Could it be on this coming December 21st? Why not? It's as good a day as any to die.

Much of the Islamic world seeks a great leader to deliver them from what they perceive to be oppression by the outside world. They particularly detest the "little Satan", Israel, and the "big Satan", good old Uncle Sam. The twelfth Imam, the Mahdi, is to return to restore justice to the world. He will not be as great as Muhammad, though in part Muhammad shall be his name. His coming is to be preceded by sixty false prophets throughout the ages. I've seen no record of how many of these have already appeared. I suspect all must have appeared by now.

Some believe that the Mahdi will appear along with the "prophet" Jesus, and together they will lead all believers to the one and only true God, Allah, and to ultimate victory over the infidels, that is essentially everyone on earth else not Muslim. Like me.

Many Muslim believers feel that there must be great chaos on earth, an Apocalypse of sorts, for the 12th Mahdi to appear. Known as devout "twelvers", the likes of Mahmoud Ahmadinejad may actually have the power (read "atom bombs") to create the chaos "needed" for the twelfth Imam to come. A nuclear holocaust would surely fit the bill. What better a day to start one than December 21, 2012?

The Jews believe the Messiah is a non-divine human being. Over millennia the Jewish people have longed for this Messiah to appear to restore the Jewish Kingdom. Some believe his presence will extend the rule of righteousness over the entire earth. The Messiah will execute judgment, and right all of man's wrongs. Many expect that he will appear soon. Could this be the year? Why not? It's as good a year as any.

Jews have long believed in this coming of a Messiah to establish a New Kingdom. The so-called "Reformed Jews" believe in the coming of a new age, the "Messianic Age", and not the actual physical arrival of a Messiah. This seems more in line with the interpretation of the Mayan calendar as perhaps prophesizing a new way of thinking, if not a "physical coming".

When Jesus was crucified the Jews of that time felt pretty bummed out. They initially believed Jesus was the anointed descendant of King David sent to them by God. Their prophesized King finally had come to deliver them from Roman oppression. He would right all wrongs, bring peace and safety, and unite their world. Oops. They're still waiting.

Once Jesus was put to death they asked: "How could Jesus be our prophesized King. He did nothing to fulfill the prophecies." They could never accept Jesus Christ as their Messiah. Most still do not, though a small group called "Jews for Jesus" apparently feel otherwise.

Of course, traditional devout Christians do accept Jesus Christ as their personal savior. The basic tenet of Christian faith is that Jesus Christ came as The Lamb of God and died in agony on the cross for the sins of all mankind. The Jewish faith does not acknowledge the Old Testament teaching that the Messiah would be put to death for mankind's sins, and be resurrected. This is the fundamental irreconcilable difference between these two faiths as I understand them. Why can't we all just get along?

So here we have a major conflict between three religions all claiming to worship the God of Abraham but from three quite different perspectives. Is there one "true God"? Whose interpretation is correct? All three lay claim to being closest to the will of God, the guardians of the true faith. It is very sad that they cannot come close to agreeing, not even amongst themselves!

I was raised in a predominately Jewish neighborhood, by a Protestant mother and an excommunicated (for marrying mom) once-devout Catholic father. I attended services at mom's Protestant church, my dad's sister's Catholic church, and often at my friends' synagogues! The understanding of Christianity that I came away with may not be traditional but it is how I was taught to believe.

I have never studied the nuanced differences between the multitude of Christian sects. What makes a Lutheran a Lutheran and a Baptist a Baptist? I haven't a clue. Nor do I particularly care. As I understood it as a child, there are simply various ways of looking at the death, resurrection, and second coming of Jesus.

The believers in heaven and hell believe that we have souls that end up one place or the other. But I was taught that when we die we all sort of go into stasis. No heaven. No hell. Nothing at all.

I was taught that Jesus will return to earth on an "appointed day" (12/21/12 ?) with 144,000 God-chosen individuals (12,000 from each of the diaspora of the so-called twelve tribes), wipe earth's slate clean of everyone else, and rule over all of earth for a thousand years. He will only THEN resurrect everyone who has ever lived before, bringing them back from their nothingness.

This will create their one and only shot at eternal bliss, "heaven" or whatever. Follow Jesus teachings to the letter and live forever. Screw up, fail to be a sheeple, and you die a second time and head back to nowhere-land forever. No heaven. No hell. Nothingness. Of course, only a third of the people on the planet believe in any of this, so maybe all the others are exempt.!

"He appointed a day in which He will judge the world." (Luke 13:3, 2Peter 3:9.) Could that day be 12/21/12? Just asking. Certainly a second coming and a slate cleaning isn't too far from the Apocalypse that I understand must happen before the twelfth Mahdi, along with the prophet Jesus, comes to rule over earth to create a blissful universal Caliphate. (As I understand Jesus' involvement with Islam's predicted "Judgment Day", He is to descend from heaven to kill the anti-Christ Dajjal, the "deceiver".)

How does a date in 2012 figure in with Muslim beliefs? In 1967, the Israeli "six-day war" reclaimed Jerusalem, a very dark day in Muslim history. That was forty-five years ago. Now let's look at the Christian Book of Daniel. Here we find a period of forty-five years, the time interval between 1290 and 1335 years (which relate to certain documented events). Though the relationship seems a bit obscure to me, this forty-five years is interpreted as an encoding figure for Islam, which, when added to 1967 gives us good old 2012! A bit of a stretch, but who am I to say.

God's Apocalypse is designed to deliver humans from their own destructive ways. It is to put an end to man's 6,000 years of lousy stewardship over earth and usher in the new era, The Kingdom of God. The ways of mankind have failed because man has rejected God's way. There will now be but one government and one religion.

All personal and business relationships will be filled with harmony and love and peace. None of this is intended to be well received by mortal man. It is intended to be God's wrath, humbling mankind as never before. We had our shot at it and blew it. 2012 Kablooie! Is this not precisely what the Mayans predict?

I address these three religions here because the "coming of Jesus" could very well be interpreted as a part of the 12/21/12 "apocalypse". For Christians, Muslims and Jews it is a "coming". Buddhists await the appearance of the "Perfect Buddha", Metteyya. The Persian teacher Zoroaster taught about a final day of judgment that would surely occur.

Hindus believe that the cosmos undergoes an infinite number of births and rebirths, and that there are infinite universes. They speak of a 12,000 year "Age of the Gods" and a 24,000 year cycle related to the equinox precession. This is quite close to the Mayan calculation of 25,627 years. How did these ancient people arrive independently at a number that pre- and post-dates their existences. No one knows. I HATE coincidences.

I wonder whether the Scientologists believe that Lord Xenu will come back again after 75 million years to do pretty much the same end-time destruction, but only to anyone who hasn't paid big bucks to be "audited" and ultimately "cleared". I've never asked one, nor do I have plans to do so! Perhaps Thomas Mopother IV knows (that is, "Tom Cruise").

In fact, I lived with a dedicated Scientologist for a few years, and aside from a few rather odd ideas and an apparent pervasive greed-motive, their basic precepts are very sound and enlightening. I've read L. Ron Hubbard's *Dianetics* a number of times and taken from it many positive thoughts. The root basis of Scientology's basic philosophy seems quite well grounded.

So just what does all this mean for 12/21/12? Well, wouldn't that be the perfect day for one of these prophesies to come true? Why not? If you are a true believer it will happen someday, why not then? Could God have tipped off the Mayans to warn us thousands of years in advance? Strange are the ways of the Lord.

I strongly believe in "God". I am not deeply religious in the church-going sense, but I do believe that some vastly superior unimaginable intelligence created this and perhaps infinite other universes. I believe this holy entity can squash us all like cockroaches at time desired. I also believe that if I were that omnipotent entity I'd be pretty damned upset at the human race on earth as a whole, and might look for a logical opportunity to start the whole thing over!

Nobody's perfect. Maybe next time around I'd get it right. So I planted this date in the Mayan consciousness to give humans lots of time to actually get it right. They didn't. Whatever. 2012 Kablooie! Next group up to the plate.

So for a moment accept the "pissed off God" hypothesis. Just what ways could the almighty wipe us all out? Any of these could happen tomorrow or any time in the future, or actually on 12/21/12.

Below follows a discussion of many possibilities, from the very possible to the very remote. I offer them simply as food for thought. I've probably missed quite a few. Any dedicated search of the internet will turn up many others.

PART FOUR

<u>COSMOLOGICAL APOCALYPSE</u>

"Self-preservation, nature's first great law; all the creatures, except man, doth awe."   Andrew Marvell, 1654.

"All the spheres revolve about the sun as their mid-point, and therefore the sun is the center of the universe." Copernicus.

A CLEAR AND ALWAYS-PRESENT DANGER

My above "Part Three", the unfathomable "holy entity" thoughts, offers "religious" ways by which earth's end could happen soon. I am going to outline below a number of possible cosmological causes of a global Apocalypse, directed by God or otherwise.

These are REAL, not imagined dangers. They are readily researched on the internet. They could happen ANY day in the future, including December 21, 2012, or never happen at all in our lifetimes. The likelihood of any one of these happening on any given day is very small, over time, almost **certain**.

I am sure that some of the material in this book will be reported out of context. "Anderson claims magic particles will destroy earth. Three physicists die laughing." You get the picture. Please be assured that no one can claim with100% certainty that any of these scenarios I offer below are impossible.

GOODBY SUN, GOODBY MILKY WAY

For starters, every astronomer knows with 100% certainty that the earth is ultimately doomed, albeit four billion years or so from now. We know the birth, life, and death cycle of stars, of which our sun is one rather unremarkable example. We know the sun will ultimately burn up its enormous store of fuel and evolve into a "red giant", swelling beyond earth's orbit. Bye bye earth and anything that happens to accidentally have survived on it to that point. This is not a worry for this coming December 21st. It will eventually happen with certainty, just not quite this particular year!

A couple of billion years before the sun fries us to a crisp, our Milky Way Galaxy is scheduled to collide with the Andromeda Galaxy. It's a sure bet. We can see and calculate its coming with precisiuon. There is no prediction possible of what might happen to our neck of the woods, but it probably won't be real pleasant. Then again, after 2012 this all could be academic.

SLOAR FLARES – "CORONAL MASS EJECTIONS"

This topic really deserves its own entire book, because it is by far the single greatest off-earth danger facing the planet today. This biggest VERY REAL problem with the sun is a phenomenon called a "coronal mass ejection", also referred to as a "solar storm" or "solar flare".

According to the June 2012 issue of National Geographic magazine, the space-weather forecast for the next few years is: "solar storms, with a chance of catastrophic blackouts". Is anyone listening? Hello government. Hello Holy men. Anyone home?

A recent report from the very highly respected National Academy of Sciences estimates that it would take **a decade and trillions of dollars** to recover from a major solar flare. A lot of ugly stuff can happen in a few months without electricity, let alone a whole decade. Karel Schrijver of Lockheed

Martin's Solar and Astrophysics Laboratory is quoted as saying: "Not preparing for it has intolerable consequences."

Stars, of which our sun is a rather unremarkable example in terms of size and temperature, are composed of a special fourth state of matter. We are all familiar with solids, liquids and gasses, but a weird fourth state called "plasma" makes up the stars. In a plasma, atoms are stripped down to naked protons and electrons.

The sun is large and hot beyond imagining. Its surface is a mere 90,000 degrees Fahrenheit. This temperature rises to two-million degrees in the sun's atmosphere (its "coronasphere") above the surface, and at the eruption point of a flare is a whopping ten-million degrees! Scientists have no idea whatsoever why these temperatures above the surface are so high. They just are.

Every second of every day the sun converts millions of tons of protons into helium nuclei. This "fusion reaction" is reported to be the equivalent energy of ten billion hydrogen bombs going off simultaneously! Yet the sun is so large that it can continue to consume itself at this rate for a few billion more years. This titanic thermonuclear furnace is not easy to comprehend. It's really, really big!

The sun has a magnetic field around it much as does the earth. The sun's magnetic field lines poke through its surface and are visible to astronomers as loops of hot glowing plasma. When loops of plasma cross they literally "short-circuit" each other causing a plasma explosion, a solar flare. Such a flare can release the energy of a billion megatons of TNT in a second!

It takes around eight minutes for photons (light) to travel from the sun to the earth. But what about the dangerous particles from a solar flare, the dreaded coronal mass ejections? This takes its good old time relative to light. In fact, it takes around two days to arrive at earth's vicinity. If a flare happens to be followed closely by a second one, this time can be cut in half because the first flare weakens earth's protective magnetic field that normally slows the particles down.

How much warning of an impending mass-ejection hit can our scientists provide? Douglas Biesker of NOAA (The National Oceanic and Atmospheric Administration) is quoted as saying: "Space weather [reporting] is where terrestrial weather [reporting] was fifty years ago." We do have two satellites, Stereo A and Stereo B, that monitor 100% of the sun's surface for flares.

And a new NOAA computer program can predict the arrival of a flare within a twelve-hour window. How comforting.

There is also an aging satellite called ACE (Advanced Composition Explorer) that monitors the "solar wind", particles leaving the sun. It can warn us of the actual intensity of a flare about to strike earth.....a whopping twenty minutes before it hits!

These solar storms have been happening for the four-plus billion years of earth's existence, but were of very little potential consequence except during the last hundred years or so of industrialized society.

The sun goes through regular "cycles" of activity, recorded peaks of excitement and quiescence separated by eleven or so years. It just so happens that this latest "solar maximum" **peaks in the general December 21, 2012 time**

frame! Not all maxima are created equal. From all indications to date this one could be an exceptionally active maximum. Coincidence? I HATE coincidences.

Inhabitants of earth are not directly threatened physically by solar flares as far as we are told. The earth's magnetosphere shields us from direct physical harm. This is a fact that public press releases from NASA and JPL love to stress: "No possible threat to humans from solar flares." What they seldom address, what they totally whitewash, is the potential for collateral damage from solar flares. They can simply kill us indirectly, and most likely will.

On September 25, 2011 an immense solar tornado, the likes of which had never before been seen, pegged at 3.6 million degrees, was observed moving rapidly across the face of the sun. Strange things were happening already, as January 2012 approached. The solar maximum was heating up (bad pun intended!).

Last April 16th one of the largest solar mass ejections ever seen blasted off into space. Fortunately it was pointed away from earth. Had it been a direct hit it might have fried every electric transformer in the grid! Earth is a ball and the sun is a ball. Both rotate. The odds of a particular spot on earth being directly in line with the exact exit point of a coronal mass ejection are not high, but they obviously do exist. We have been VERY lucky to date.

Solar flares, coronal mass ejections, are numerically rated: one rated "c (with a number following)" is weak and harmless; "m (#)" medium and potentially dangerous; and "x (#)" powerful and deadly. If a single "very-high x#" flare makes a direct hit on the United States and Canada we are all literally toast. Or at least the electric grid is. We are survivors sans electricity. We become cavepersons once again. And it CAN happen this solar cycle.

On March 17, 2012 at 1:15 PM, Accuweather.com ran an absolutely moronic video on their website. Its title was: "Could A Solar Flare Destroy Earth?" The moderator was an idiotic-looking dude in a shiny wide-brimmed tin-hat that looked like anupside-down cuspidor! Ha, ha, ha! Clearly they were making this "solar flare" thing into a big joke. One could tell immediately that the message was going to be: "Of course not, you idiots".

This nincompoop went on to mention the "solar maximum" that we are entering. He asked glibly: "Could The Earth Really Be Destroyed?" "Is The End in sight?" Then he offhandedly and very briefly mentioned some possible effect on the power grid, but stated unequivocally that no harm could come to people or to the earth itself from any solar flare. Really?

He did mention correctly that we would have a two to three day advance warning before any flare arrives once spotted on the sun's surface. At 193,000,000 miles or so away it takes a while for the particles from a solar flare to reach our planet. Advance warning is good. Two days advance warning is not good enough.

Mr. Tin Hat then glibly added what a great benefit to humanity a major solar flare would be. We could all see the beautiful auroras created above our poles once the particles reach earth's magnetosphere! I just can't wait. The video was taken down permanently after just a few hours. Curious.

Writer Patrick Geryl (see Bibliography) seems convinced that the sun's current hyper-activity will result in a reversal in our home star's magnetic poles. This will cause massive high-number-X-class solar flares, huge coronal mass ejections stronger than ever witnessed before. This in turn will reverse earth's magnetic poles causing massive planet-wide earthquakes, volcanos and tsunamis wiping out seven-billion or so earthlings on December 21st. Astronomers tend to not agree. 2012 Kablooie?

Solar flares do cause a measurable fluctuation in earth's protective magnetosphere. Such fluctuations can in fact induce high currents in power lines, telephone wires, and cable networks. This is a known fact. On September 2, 1859 a large solar flare slammed into earth. It overpowered the magnetosphere, and caused havoc to the state-of-the-art technology of the day.

Telegraph wires were fried throughout the United States and Europe! Many fires were ignited. These telegraph wires are analogous to today's electrical transmission lines. And this one was FAR from the most powerful flare possible.

In just the past decade there have been around twenty large solar flares strike the earth. All were less than one-quarter the strength of the 1859 flare. In the past half century there have been five major strikes. One in 1958 caused over a hundred Europe-to-United States planes to lose radio contact with the ground. In a 1972 coronal mass ejection event a transformer in British Columbia actually exploded!

The flare that totally shut down the Eastern Canadian power grid on March

13, 1989 was just a wee baby compared to the size flare that is theoretically possible. This one was only about one-third as powerful as the 1859 flare. In two minutes six-million Canadians found themselves temporarily back in the stone-age!

In 2000 the ASCA research satellite lost navigational control due to a solar flare. In 2003 Sweden was blacked out and the Global Positioning System failed, all due to relatively minor solar coronal mass ejections.

In relative terms, on an index that measures the disturbance in our magnetic field caused by a solar flare, the 1859 event was an "850". Anything over 300 is considered "extreme", like the 1989 event. A moderate flair indexes at 150. A 1,000+ flare? 2012 Kablooie! It is very far from impossible.

Want a real example of how fragile an electric grid is? On April 4, 2012 the entire COUNTRY of Cyprus lost 100% of its electric power because of a relatively minor electric-system part failure! Not a solar event, but an example of just how fragile a power grid can be.

Remember the "Big Blackout" on the East Coast of the USA many decades ago? That, too, was caused by a relatively minor failure in a single item resulting in a "cascade" effect of grid shutdowns.

I happened to be on an upper floor of a CCNY college building taking an MBA night class at the exact time the entire city of New York went black. We filed down a number of staircases in total darkness, which took about ten minutes. The trek was punctuated by giggles and screams as various jokesters goosed whoever happened to be in front of them!

But what amazed me the most, as we finally emerged from the building, was the incredible sight of individuals on the street already selling flashlights at ten bucks a pop! Entrepreneurship really flourished back then. Capitalism at its finest!

As with the predicted "big one" earthquake overdue to hit California, the "big one" solar flare is very overdue. Nothing equivalent to the 1859 flare has happened recently, and that's over a hundred-fifty year period. Even that flare was not even close to the maximum flare that is theoretically possible.

A recent report from the prestigious U. S. National Academy of Sciences estimated that a large coronal mass ejection happening these days would cause many trillions of dollars in damage. It would totally paralyze modern earth, fueling chaos around the world, with recovery taking decades! The result would be unthinkable. 2012 Kablooie?

For most "average" solar flares even a few hours advanced notice allows operators of satellites and power stations time to make "switch-off " provisions. They do have time needed to make the many relatively-easy preparations necessary to protect their sensitive systems. But for the "Big One", there are NO possible preparations that they CAN make. There is no way to protect hundreds of satellites, tens of thousands of transformers, and millions of miles of exposed transmission wires. No way at all.

Of course there is some level of protection in place at most power plants, in the form of replacement transformers, known as "backup redundancy". Sadly there is no government mandate requiring 100% transformer redundancy. It is up to each individual power plant. There should be such a government mandate. The power plants "can't afford redundancy".

Would it not be a better use of "stimulus" funds to subsidize purchase of backup transformers to create 100% redundancy to preserve our electric grid? What about spending that money setting up huge food-storage depots, much as some cities actually did prior to the Y2K non-event? Think of the jobs this would create. Should this not be at least a splinter in the political planks of the major political parties? Will it be? Or course not. What is so important about the end of society as we know it?

The big unknown is the effect of a truly huge solar flare on the millions of miles of exposed power lines. Because it has never happened to date, no one can say for sure just what the effect would actually be. Those in the know say it won't be pretty.

In a perfect world all of our electric distribution wires would be underground. Aside from solar flare protection, this would also preclude downed wires from major windstorms, such as happened last June. Many millions in ten states were without power for many days due to trees that downed above-ground lines. The problem with this is, as always, cost. It is estimated to cost five to fifteen million dollars a mile to place existing transmission wires underground. Is our survival worth it?

A solar- fried grid could eventually be rebuilt, but it might take years, even decades. The unlucky "powerless" country on the side of earth that is hit directly by a mega-flare would be totally vulnerable to attack and occupation from anyone on the "relatively lucky" side of the planet which might not sustain as much damage. Think China. Think Mid-East. How's your Mandarin? Farsi anyone?

Can any good come from a solar flare? Well, aurora are very beautiful to see! These are produced when solar particles react with earth's magnetosphere, its electric field. Electrons are literally pushed down into earth's atmosphere along magnetic field lines. Upon contact, atmospheric gases are "excited", giving off light and color. In the 1859 flare event aurora were reportedly visible from Hawaii and Cuba! Nice.

On last July 2nd a "look for the beautiful aurora" alert was issued! A massive solar flare was on its way. Fortunately this one was not expected to be a direct hit but just a glancing blow on earth's ionosphere. Things are literally just beginning to heat up (bad pun) and scientists are becoming **very** concerned to say the least.

Economics aside, now, this very day, you have good reason for procuring some sort of solar-powered electrical backup at your home. Screw the grid. It's too fragile. If you can afford it, being totally "off grid" with solar panels or a wind turbine makes immense sense. At the very least buy a small solar-powered electric generator. These are commercially available, and not terribly expensive. If you are living in a rural location and have your own water-well, a solar-powered well-pump is also a great idea.

The very sun that could fry the electrical grid permanently could save your life. Don't rely on someone selling you flashlights and batteries after the fact! (See the Appendix below.)

COMETS, ASTEROIDS, AND OTHER SPACE-OBJECTS

Let's shift focus to something that is absolutely true. Earth is a tiny ball of rock in a very big galaxy floating in a vast cosmos. Every single minute of every day we are bombarded by particles of matter from space. These can be anything from tiny primordial dust to larger fragments thrown off by impacts between various bodies in space, to the dirty balls of ice and rock we call comets.

The vast majority of these dust, ice and rock particles burn up in our atmosphere. At least half of the time these are unseen, because half of the planet is in daylight! They are seen on the night side only if they are around pea-size or larger when then enter our atmosphere. These leave a trail of "shooting star" light, we call a meteor. They are fun to watch.

Occasionally a piece is large enough to make it to the surface before it burns away and is found on the ground as a "meteorite". This happened last May in California, and touched off a "gold rush" of rockhounds seeking valuable (to collectors and scientists) pieces right on the surface of the ground.

Interesting aside fact: when a meteorite lands on earth, after its fiery journey through our atmosphere, it is ice-cold! Starting in space's near absolute-zero degrees the heating caused by friction with our atmosphere does not overcome the meteorite's internal "super-coldness".

The potential serious problem for earthlings is that there are much larger space rocks lurking out there by the millions. The vast majority never come anywhere near to earth. But some do. A few thousand years ago one hit near Yucatan and is believed to have led, directly or otherwise, to the demise of the dinosaurs. A similar hit today would probably wipe out most of humanity.

But, you say, don't we have sophisticated instruments that detect these rocks long before they ever pose a threat? Well, yes and no. The fact is that at this writing we do NOT even have a totally accurate asteroid-threat **census**! We simply do not have the funding for the needed research that could save the planet. We have more pressing priorities, such as lavish parties in Vegas for government groups. So we really do not know what degree of danger is out there from potentially catastrophic collisions.

Compared to the trillions of dollars we manage to piss away each year, or give to governments around the globe that hate us, we need to allocate just a few million dollars to the study of asteroids that could annihilate the planet. Bad prioritizing. What else is new?

We do have lots of instruments attempting to locate and track these NEOs, or Near Earth Objects. But clearly they are far from infallible, and need some serious upgrading. Cases in point:

Let's look at some facts: On April 1, 2012, a rock about a hundred-fifty feet wide passed between the earth and the moon. The scary thing is that it was first detected just thirteen days before it almost hit earth!   A rock this size would at the very least create a shock wave in the atmosphere that could level hundreds of square miles. If it happened over a big city that city would be toast. This puppy was designated 2012EG5.

But that was a "far miss" compared to 2012FS3S which passed within only

36,000 miles of earth on March 26th a week earlier. In astronomical terms that is a VERY near miss. On that same day an even larger rock, the size of a large bus, 2012FP3S, missed by 96,000 miles. Shortly thereafter space rock FA57 passed just outside the moon's orbit. That's four close ones in just a month! Ever hear about any of this in the media? I doubt it.

Scary enough already?   How's this for scary? On May 29th NASA made a startling announcement. Of course it got zero press coverage. They announced the results of the most detailed survey to date of "PHAs" (Potentially Hazardous Asteroids). They reported that NASA recently discovered 4,700 of these dangerous space rocks zipping around out there and potentially threatening earth!

Further, they have determined that the number of these killers that are inclined in their orbits in such a way that their eventual strike on earth is far more probable than originally thought is double their previous estimates. The biggest problem is that we just do not detect these in time to do anything about them, even if we had the deflection technology imagined in various Hollywood flicks.

Case In Point: On Tuesday, May 29, 2012, with less than 24 hours advance warning, an asteroid (dubbed 2012KT42) whizzed by at an incredibly close 9,000 miles! That's just a touch more than the distance from New York to Tokyo!

Had this rock, travelling at fifteen miles per second or so (that's 54,000 mph!) hit Central Park in New York City or downtown Tokyo it would have wiped out millions of people in an instant! Was this widely reported in the press? If it was, I couldn't find it. How lucky

were we earthlings this time? **VERY**.
December 21st? We'll see.

Ah, but you say, the earth is huge, and
the chances of an asteroid hitting a big
city is statistically small. That is very
true. But what if it hits a statistically
much more likely target, the ocean? Big
splash! How about "big splash equals a
massive tsunami"? Just how massive
would of course depend on the size of
the object striking water, where it struck,
and the angle of strike, but it is a
certainty that there could be massive
numbers of coastal human casualties.
Glub.

Another real danger is the gut human
reaction to any large asteroid strike.
Would the nation where it landed be
convinced they were under nuclear
attack and immediately launch a
retaliation against some innocent
"enemy"? That is certainly not beyond

the realm of possibility in our nuclear-jittery world.

Not long ago a glitch in Russia's missile detection system indicated an incoming strike from a United States based Intercontinental Ballistic Missile. Fortunately the Russian technician with his finger on the retaliation button had the good sense to recheck the viability of the signal. Whew! Close one.

Scientist Adam Garde, a senior research scientist with the Geological Survey of Denmark and Greenland, recently made a startling discovery. Studying maps in his Copenhagen office he noticed a correlation between strange geologic features in West Greenland and odd concentrations of nickel and platinum. After studying aerial photos it has been concluded that there is an ancient sixty-two mile wide (!) meteoric impact crater formed by a massive object that was **nineteen miles**

wide! They report that should a similar object hit earth today it would destroy all higher live….that is, us. Food for thought.

The fact is, earth is a space-target with a bulls-eye on it.   The important fact is that the media never tells us much about any of this. You have to dig pretty deep to find any mention at all. Here's food for thought: Let's say "they" knew for certain that we were about to all be vaporized by a huge space object, say for example on December 21st. Would we be told in advance, risking world-wide panic? I doubt it. Why bother?

Are there any actual predictions of a really big asteroid hit in our lifetimes? Well, on June 19, 2004 a large object, astronomers named Apophis, was first detected. Its exact size is still unknown. Its orbit is continuously refined by our instruments , but at this writing there is a real possibility that it could hit earth on

April 13, 2029. Could the Mayans have been off by sixteen years or so? 2029 Kablooie?

If there is a near miss in 2029, which could be by just a few thousand miles, the next time around in its orbit, there is almost a certainty it will hit earth in 2098. Most of us won't be around for that one! Of course, assuming we get past 12/21/12, by 2098 we should have the technology to deflect an object of almost any size. The point to all of this is that there is ALWAYS the very real possibility we could be wiped out by an unwelcome massive visitor from space.

Although comets are almost universally believed to be porous dirty space-snowballs, not solid rocks as are most asteroids, they can still be dangerous. Around 650 AD it is believed that a comet fragment that hit Britain led to seven years of perpetual winter and

eventually to the European "Dark Ages".
That was one really big nasty snowball!

Consider the real need for an infallible
"space-debris defense system". To date
no country has even an earth-missile
defense system that is 100% effective.
Israel claims to be able to kill 80% of the
rockets that rain down upon them
almost daily from their Islamic buddies
next door. That's not too comforting if
you happen to be at ground zero for the
other 20%! And the vastly underfunded
USA missile defense system isn't even
close to that of Israel. Comforting? Is
anyone listening? Probably not.
The same is true for asteroids. OK, let's
say astronomers find most of them far in
advance. The recent twenty-four hours
warning isn't too comforting. What
about **one** hour? Can a single
devastating space rock out of millions
sneak in under the radar? Apparently
the answer is: "Yes!". Of course the

government "experts" will say: "No!".
We are in no possible clear and present
danger from large space-rocks, right?
We never are. Just ask JPL and NASA.

NIBIRU - THE PLANET THAT PROBABLY ISN'T

There is one Apocalypse theory that has
absolutely been proven to be untrue, or
so you will be told. This is the supposed
existence of Nibiru, a mysterious planet
ostensibly hidden from our view behind
the sun or simply somehow invisible.
It's just sitting there ready to pounce on
December 21st.

The actual concept of a planet called
"Nibiru" was first brought to our attention
by the late author Zacharia Stitchen in
his book "The 12th Planet". It was
based on his interpretation of an ancient
Sumerian text that had this massive
object coming back to earth's
neighborhood every 3,600 years or so.

This book of Stitchen's was translated into dozens of languages and incredibly sold millions of copies. And there are many millions of believers in the existence of Nibiru. The "ground zero" date predicted many years ago is in late 2012!

Apparently one of the "believers" in a large invisible planet was Hunbatz Men, a present-era Mayan "Daykeeper" I mentioned earlier. He taught a course ten years ago about a planet called Tzoltze ek' by the Maya, which is the Sumerian-postulated planet Nibiru. His lectures surely added fuel to the Mayan Apocalypse interpretations.

Well, Tzoltze ek' or Nibiru apparently ain't there! We've seen "behind" the sun from our satellites in space. We've seen the far reaches of space. Nothing of planetary size is seen lurking there waiting for December 21st to blast our planet into oblivion. Forget Tzoltze ek' and Nibiru. Not happening. That is, at least not as a "planet" in the conventional sense. But what about the un-conventional?

What if this planet is actually somehow invisible? We cannot "see" dark-matter, and we cannot "see" black holes. We know they exist from the effects they have on other bodies in space. Could there be an as yet unknown and "un-seeable" large object composed of something presently unknown to science? Your guess is as good as mine.

As recently as the June 2012 issue of Astronomy magazine it was pointed out that astronomers do in fact believe that there are BILLIONS of rogue planets in the cosmos. These are planets not orbiting any star, just drifting aimlessly through space. In fact, it is postulated that more of them may exist than stars themselves! This has been deduced by astronomers from gravitational "lensing" effects noted while studying the center of our galaxy.

Did the ancient Mayans or Sumerians know something that our astronomers have only learned within the past few years? Who tipped them off? "Fascinating", as Star Trek's Mr. Spock would say.

Also, could Tzoltze ek' or Nibiru actually exist but be somehow "cloaked"? It's there but we cannot see it for some reason or other? In Star Trek certain civilizations invented "cloaking devices" that could render entire massive starships invisible. Harry Potter had his "cloak of invisibility". Visionary imaginings by Gene Roddenberry and J. K. Rowling? Here's the astonishing truth. We humans have recently actually created real cloaking devices here on earth!

Check it out on the internet. Cloaking devices, even different types of them, are no longer only theoretical. We have actually demonstrated them! It is not at all hard to extrapolate our current fledgling cloaking technology into something on a vastly larger scale by a civilization only a few hundred or thousands of years more advanced than ours. A cloaked planet? One never knows. Except perhaps the Mayans and the Sumerians.

WEIRD PHYSICS

To me, the most amazing fact is that astronomers and physicists are convinced that the vast majority of the known universe is made up of something they have dubbed "dark matter" and "dark energy". They know they are there from the gravitational effects exerted by dark matter and the galaxy-repulsive force exerted by dark energy, but they cannot see either or measure them directly. They simply do not don't know what they are, and they account for almost everything. Astounding level of scientific ignorance!

Astronomers and physicists have dubbed dark matter particles "WIMPS". It is an acronym for: "Weakly Interactive Massive Particles". Many credible scientists believe that we are constantly bombarded by WIMPS, and that they continuously pass through our bodies and our planet every day leaving no ill effects at all. Creepy! Is that what gives me an occasional tingling sensation? Nah, that's just old age.

Why is this relevant? Well, for one thing these are the same "all knowing" experts who are telling you that there is nothing going on that could possibly harm you in late December. They do not know diddily-squat about what the entire universe is made up of yet they are experts in what cannot possibly happen to us! That in itself does not give me the warm fuzzies.

These same folk know with certainty that our entire Milky Way Universe has two immense gamma ray bubbles emanating from the galactic center. They are well-defined bubbles and easily detected. Their creation had to have been by way of some unimaginably energetic event, yet astronomers don't have a clue what created them. Just add this to the long list of scientists' "don't have a clues". But we are surely safe from any harm from beyond earth. Just ask the experts.

In fact, I can predict with 100% certainty that every physicist on earth will read much of what follows below and at best get a chuckle out of it. At worst, there will be all-knowing guarantees that these sorts of things are absolutely, totally, and theoretically impossible. So let's see if we can piss off a few physicists just for fun!

How about the Higgs Boson, the so-called "God Particle"? That's the final piece of the grand puzzle for particle physicists. Until they find it they have sleepless nights because without it their various calculations don't quite explain "everything". That's right up there with dark matter and dark energy. The process itself of looking for this tiny bugger has some scientists believing that destructive "black holes" could happen accidentally and kill us all!

In late June it was excitedly announced that this God Particle was finally found....sort of. Scientists say they have discovered its "footprint", but they have not actually seen the particle itself. It has very tiny feet!

Anti-matter is another amazing but very real curiosity. One dilemma facing astro-physicists is why, when the universe was created, there were not equal amounts of matter and anti-matter created. Of course if there were, everything would cancel out and there would be no physicists to study it! Could there be clouds of anti-matter lurking around out there waiting to anti-earth? Who knows for certain? Certainly not the scientists.

In fact, as recently as 2010 scientists actually created anti-matter at Brookhaven National Laboratory on Long Island, New York. Using the "Relativistic Heavy Ion Collector" they created a previously unknown type of matter they dubbed an "anti-hypertriton". It simply annihilates absolutely any other regular matter with which it comes in contact. Let's hope they don't make too much of the stuff!

Let's take "black holes" as another example of "real but weird". They are known to exist, with 100% scientific certainty. These are unimaginably dense assemblages of matter that exert so much gravitational force that even light itself cannot escape (which is, not coincidentally, why they are black!)

They tend to gobble up anything in their vicinity. And they come in all sizes. What would happen if a little bitty undetectable black hole just happened to drop by earth? And on December 21st. 2012 Kablooie?

No one knows what would happen if such a black hole were actually to hit earth because there is no possible experiment to show what the effect might be. In fact, it is reported that some scientists believe that the "Tunguska Event", a huge flattened forest in Russia from ages ago, was caused by one such item, a tiny black hole, striking earth. Most believe it was a comet strike, which isn't all that much more comforting.

And then there is the "Majorana Fermion" particle? I've asked a few physicist friends about that one and I get a blank stare. When one of these little puppies finds itself a nice fat positron, POOF! An instantaneous annihilation event occurs in a flash of gamma rays. Now I'm not suggesting that there are unknown numbers of little majorana-fermion particles, tiny time-bombs, floating around out there in space waiting to destroy earth. Any particle physicist will say: "impossible". You must remember, this is a "what if" book! Impossible? No one can say for certain.

Just a few years ago scientists discovered some REALLY weird stuff. Can the same item exist in two places at the same time? Intuitively of course not, but apparently so! Can the motion of one item create a similar motion in the other one even though they are very far apart, even miles apart? Yes indeed! Quantum mathematicians call this phenomenon "entanglement". It is very real, and is being studied intensely as you read this.

On a galactic, or cosmologic scale, it gets even weirder. Many PhD physicists believe in the possibility of the existence of infinite "bubble universes" of which our cosmos is simply one example. Can bubble universes collide? What if one bubble universe is composed primarily of anti-matter in the same fashion that our cosmos somehow favors matter? 2012 Kablooie?

And then there are "branes" and "strings", other very seriously postulated alternative universes. Are they dangerous? Only the Great Creator knows for sure. What about "nested universes"? There is a theory that there is an infinite hierarchy of universes in infinite upwards and downwards progressions and regressions. Shrink down to electron size, and what do you find? Another full-blown universe! As with the big and little frogs eating one another rhyme's ending: "....and so on infinitum."

NASA has acknowledged that the most powerful explosions in the cosmos are those that release deadly gamma rays. The amount of energy released in a few milliseconds exceeds the amount of energy our sun would release in its entire ten-billion-year lifetime! Astronomers believe that a galaxy called WR104 is positioned to direct one of these bursts at earth. Such an event is predicted to have occurred there some time in the last 8,000 years. If it happened fully 8,000 years ago it could arrive tomorrow! Or on December 21st. They further predict that the arrival of these gamma rays would extinguish all life on earth in a heartbeat! How comforting.

Lastly, we always have the real and present danger of an unseen and undetectable x-ray burst from a cataclysm in some galaxy far, far away. We know these bursts happen. We see a few each year. To date, in our lifetimes, none has occurred in a relatively nearby star within our own Milky Way Galaxy. We are not entirely certain why, nor can we predict the effect on our lives should a really big one happen to hit earth spot on from a "local" star.

These galactic cataclysms creating massive x-ray events are called "super-novae". The excrement of exploding suns, these dangerous x-ray particles are emitted from an explosion so bright that a single exploding star in a galaxy millions of light years away shines for a day or so with greater brightness than all of the other billions of stars in its host galaxy COMBINED! What if a relatively nearby star within the Milky Way galaxy decides to go supernovae? Think VERY dark toast. 2012 Kablooie in spades!

What I am trying to share with you here is that there are many, many things going on in the universe that we do not yet fully understand, cannot control, and certainly cannot predict. Is the instantaneous mutual annihilation of real particles worth worrying about? X-ray bursts? Black holes? Anti-matter? Rogue planets? Who knows? But no one can say with certainty that we are entirely safe. Least of all the government!

PART FIVE

<u>NATURAL PLANETARY PHENOMENA</u>

"We can only conclude that it is too much to ask of us poor twentieth-century humans to think, to believe, to grasp the possibility that the system might fail. We cannot grasp the simple and elementary fact that this technology can blow a fuse." News commentary after the 1965 East Coast Blackout.

PALANTARY FLIP-FLOP

Perhaps our biggest "Apocalypse" problem stems from the media and TV ads making a joke out of the whole "end-of-time" scenario. For example, TD Ameritrade runs an ad that blurts: "If you believe the Mayan calendar says that on 12/21 the earth's poles will reverse and we'll all get tossed into space (blah, blah)......but if you are still around on 12/22 then you still need our financial services blah, blah, blah".

The point is, the Mayan calendar-end doesn't prophesize anything of the kind! This sort of "for public consumption" crap just perpetuates the "joke" and implies, by being absurd, that the entire matter is laughable. It truly isn't.

Some have postulated that the earth's axis is going to shift suddenly on December 21st, which I'm told by local professional astronomers is quite impossible. I live near both Kitt Peak and Smithsonian Observatories in Arizona and visit them often to talk with the pros. They tell me that the orbit of the moon around the earth stabilizes earth's axis. The earth's poles flip and we all fall off? Not hardly.

Another group of doomsayers believe that the gravitational effects of some rare alignment of the planets, earth, sun and moon and the entire Milky Way galaxy itself is going to cause a massive tidal wave that will inundate the earth on December 21st. Even if such an alignment occurred, which it does occasionally, as Carl Sagan humorously pointed out in "*Cosmos*", the obstetrician delivering a baby has more gravitational effect on mom than do the moon and all the planets combined. Why? Because he's a hell of a lot closer!

And earth's magnetic field? Yes, it does actually reverse every five-hundred-thousand years or so. Geologists can tell that from the orientation of magnetic particles in ancient rocks. For starters, it is not an instantaneous event. Even if it were, aside from screwing up compasses, there is no way imaginable that life on the planet would be adversely affected.

VOLCANOS AND SUPER-VOLCANOS

Now here is something over which we should get at least a little worried. There are many volcanos on earth that are quite active at any given moment. They are responsible for more air pollution and global warming in a week than all of the cars on earth in a lifetime!

I lived on the Big Island of Hawaii for six years within a short drive of Kilauea Volcano, which has been spewing out lava and noxious gasses for decades. Aside from creating "vog", Hawaii's answer to LA's "smog", it's pretty to watch but harmless unless you happen to fall Gollum-like into the caldera!

It is a fact that a brand new Hawaiian Island is being created east of the Big Island as I write this. Lo'ihi is rapidly building an undersea dome of hardened lava that is now just 963 meters or so from its top to the surface. This will be the next and easternmost Hawaiian Island at some time in the future.

Undersea volcanos are very common. In fact, it is reported that there may be over five-thousand of them worldwide!

Major volcanic activity seems to be increasing at an alarming rate as we approach December 21st. It is the land-based volcanos we see and feel and best understand. Mexico's Popocateptl, between Mexico City and Puebla , is pouring out gas and ash as I write this. A mere 25,000,000 people live within just sixty miles of the caldera!

Last November a 100-year volcanic event occurred in central Africa. In the Democratic Republic of the Congo, Mount Nyamulagira had a major eruption event, threatening the major city of Goma. Is all of this current activity a coincidence?

On the island of Sicily, just last January, Italy's famous Mount Etna once again began pouring out a massive column of ash. As of last June 1st there had been five separate major Etna eruptions in 2012.

In fact, there are no fewer than twenty-nine (29!) active, gas and ash spewing volcanos on earth today. Did you know that? Until I researched it I didn't have a clue. You never read about them.

This one fact alone makes the entire "man-made global warming" issue a bit of a joke. In one month these twenty-nine account for more air particulate and noxious gas pollution than all the fossil-fueled power plants on the planet do in our lifetime! Sorry, Greenies, you can't legislate away a volcano.

And there are at least seventy (70!) other volcanos on earth that are known to have the real potential for eruption much sooner than later, not including those deep beneath the oceans. Indonesia alone is said to have over four-hundred potential future major eruption sites.

We never hear about these events because they are only newsworthy if you happen to live near one. The "Morning News" from Vanuatu or Paupa New Guinea, let alone the Sangihe Islands, doesn't often make page one of your local rag. We tend to think of these events as every-day earth-happenings. No big deal, right? And for the most part, air pollution aside, they are not. Usually.

On May 8, 1902 about 30,000 people died at Saint-Pierre, Martinique, when the Mount Pelee volcano erupted unexpectedly.   A huge flow of hot gas and rock and mud, known as a "pyroclastic flow", burst from the summit and flowed outward with devastating consequences to the island's inhabitants. To this day similar eruptions are generically dubbed: "Palean Eruptions".

The beautiful island of Montserrat in the Caribbean was known for years as "The Emerald Isle". No longer. That was so until 2007 when a massive inactive volcano erupted in the Soufriere Hills rendering most of this beautiful island uninhabitable to this very day. This event was neither predicted nor expected.

But every rare so often something different and even more violent happens. Consider the "Mount St. Helens" eruption in 1980. The better part of a large mountain in Washington State unexpectedly popped its cork. In a heartbeat half of a mountain disappeared. The eruption flattened the neighborhood for miles around.

It killed a few unlucky souls who happened to be in the immediate vicinity eating a picnic lunch and enjoying a cold brewski at the time. But even this violent event was puny compared to at least two we know of that occurred in the relatively recent past, geologically speaking.

About four-thousand years ago a massive eruption occurred near Santorini, Greece. What scientists say is extraordinary about that event was that the volcano had been virtually dormant for 180 centuries before. Surprise!!!

Far greater even than the Santorini event was the eruption of Mount Krakatau, (better known as "Krakatoa") near Sumatra, in 1115 AD.   Dormant thereafter for another 768 years, in August 1883 it unexpectedly erupted with the greatest force ever recorded by man's instruments. It is credited with producing the loudest "bang" ever heard by humans on earth before or since!

Its power is said to have been the equivalent of 26 hydrogen bombs being exploded simultaneously! The resulting tsunami, a 100+ foot wall of water, killed 36,000 unlucky coastal dwellers. That is one hell of an explosion! It is still active to this day, spawning "Anak Krakatau" or "Child of Krakatau".

Believe it or not these colossal eruptions are themselves puny alongside the infrequent "super-volcano" eruptions. These occur roughly once every fifty-thousand years, luckily for us.

Some 73,500 years ago geologists report that the largest volcanic explosion within the past twenty-million years occurred in Sumatra. It merely deposited a ten feet deep layer of ash as far away as India! It filled earth's atmosphere with sulfur dioxide resulting in a rain of sulfuric acid that wiped out most of earth's living creatures at the time. Today's Lake Toba is all that remains in evidence.

Prior to that event there was a super-volcano eruption right here in the United States. There is a unique seventy square mile region around Lake Mono in California. It shows geologists that back a million or so years ago an eruption almost as large as the later one that formed Lake Toba occurred here. Then over the past 40,000 years, and as recently as 1300 AD, this potential future-mega-disaster super-volcano continued to erupt periodically.

This area, plus a frightening bulging dome under Yellowstone Park in Wyoming, may present the greatest real and present dangers to human life on the planet today. Should there be massive crustal plate shifts, or massive earthquakes caused by whatever (fracking?), it is almost a certainty that the unimaginable fury of these super-volcanos would be unleashed. 2012 Kablooie?

Professional volcanologist Dr. Guilherme Gualda of Vanderbilt University states: "Our study suggests that when these exceptionally large magma pools form they are ephemeral and cannot exist very long without erupting". "The fact that the process of magma body formation occurs in historical time, instead of geologic time, completely changes the nature of the problem." He defines "ephemeral" as lasting as little as 500 years before eruption. We may be well overdue for the next "big one".

What's the point of all this? Well, for one thing, although volcanologists today have all manner of sensitive instruments both on the ground and on satellites in orbit used in an effort to predict eruptions of dormant or prospective volcanos, it is far from an exact science.

It is known for certain, just as with the one that lurks just below Yellowstone Park, that there are many massive domes of magma close to earth's surface just itching to escape.

Some say when, not if, these blow, it will make Krakatoa and Santorini look like firecrackers. It could even exceed the Lake Nomo and Lake Toba events. Bye bye Western USA, and the rest of life on earth! 2012 Kablooie?

Many of the "pole shift" and "magnetic field reversal" folk believe that events, which some consider inevitable and even probable on December 21st, will trigger many such super-volcanoes worldwide. It is easy to say "hogwash", as the government of course will say, but it is clearly not beyond possibility, if not on 12/21/12 than certainly some day in the near future.

TSUNAMIS

We only need to look back at recent past history, to Indonesia and Japan, to get some idea of what devastation a relatively small tsunami, or "tidal wave", can cause. In fact, some "2012 Apocalypse" writers are imploring their readers to move to much higher ground, expecting a massive tsunami on December 21st that will wipe out anything located below, say, five-thousand feet above mean sea level! These folk are quite serious. But what could cause such a massive tsunami?

The general cause of most tsunamis is the up-thrusting of earths crustal plates as they slide and grind across each other in the endless re-positioning of earth's land masses. We live on a thin crust of rock that floats on a viscous molten sea liquid rock. The earth is cooling. The crust is shrinking and shriveling.

Sometimes when a crustal plate beneath the ocean slips by another, creating an earthquake, there is little or no uplifting of either crustal plate, and no tsunami results. When the plates slide side by side, you'll get an earthquake, but no big tsunami. If one plate thrusts upward a bit, you get a tsunami.

But what if, just once, and for whatever reason, one plate decides to blast almost straight up a long way into the miles-high column of water above it. The resultant tsunami would surely equal or far exceed Noah's flood! One author has even suggested that civilization's only hope is (was its only hope; it's too late now if you believe 12/21/12 is THE day) to build huge waterproof ships to ride out the end-of-the-world tsunami.

Another possible cause of a mighty tidal wave is the collapse of a large chunk of continental shelf into the ocean. For example, the lava shelf being added to daily off Hawaii Island by the active Kilauea volcano is a perfect example. In that case, it is not a matter of "if" but "when" it actually cracks off, plunges into the ocean, and makes a massive splash. How large a wave will occur? No one knows, but some scientists believe it could be catastrophic worldwide.

And of course huge volcanic eruptions such as Krakatoa, with water rushing in to fill the hole left behind after a few cubic miles of terra firma are sent skyward, can create unimaginably high waves that can travel around the entire globe.

Lastly, should a major piece of space rock, asteroid or comet or whatever, strike water and not strike land (which is quite likely since most of earth's surface is water) the resultant tidal wave is incalculable. As mentioned earlier, it would simply be a matter of how big a piece of rock, and at what angle it struck, and where.

For those who would find a biblical reference comforting (!) look at Matthew 24: 36-39. It speaks of the suddenness of the last great flood:

"No one knows about that day or hour, not even the angels in heaven nor the Son but only the Father. As it was in the days of Noah so it will be at the coming of the Son of Man. For in the days before the flood people were eating and drinking and giving in marriage up to the day Noah entered the ark. And they knew nothing about what would happen until the flood came and took them all away. That is how it will be at the coming of the Son of Man."

In today's world, we'll all be tweeting and fornicating and watching "American

Idol", and then, without warning, 2012 Kablooie! I hate prophecies. The problem with them is that somewhere along the line one might just come true.

EARTHQUAKES

In the past few years the incidence of major earthquakes seems to have increased. Is this leading up to "The Big One"? Here again, the answer is not if, but when. The day may come when people in Arizona and Nevada have ocean-front property! A massive movement in California's San Andreas fault, the juncture of two massive crustal plates, is considered by expert geologists to be over a hundred years overdue.

We hear of a "7.8" earthquake and know it was a large potentially destructive one. If you heard later that it was "actually a 8.0" would you think that indicated almost the same intensity?

Probably you would, but it is far from the same. ~~EACH 0.1 unit added equals TEN TIMES the destructive energy!~~ ~~Thus~~ An 8.0 earthquake is ~~100~~ 32 times more powerful than an ~~7.0~~. A 9.0 is 1000 Times more Powerful ! One need look no further than Japan in 2010, and the resulting tsunami and nuclear generating plant meltdown, to see what   devastation a moderately-large earthquake can cause.

If we play "what if", the power of a 10.0 earthquake, should it ever happen, could literally, by definition, wipe out everything. Total destruction. Possible?   In theory, yes, most definitely. Ready to happen on December 21st? The pole-shift folk sure think so.

TORNADOS AND HURRICANES (AND DERECHOS!)

Statistically, we are in a recent age of very unusual weather. We see thousands of temperature records fall almost monthly. In fact, an unprecedented 40,000 daily-high temperature records in the United States were eclipsed in the first six months of 2012!

We see massive hail storms and off-the-chart numbers of tornados, at least in the United States. Late March 2012 saw an unprecedented number of tornados devastate and kill. In fact in May a rare tornado even struck a suburb of Tokyo! In late June a rare and massive "derecho" horizontal windstorm devastated much of the Eastern United States.

Blame it all on global warming (the real uncontrollable kind, not the fantasized man-made kind) or solar activity or whatever, these recent weather-related anomalies are a statistical fact. "Strange things are happening", as the late Soupy Sales would say. Those who see "The End" on the near horizon point to these weather anomalies as the first "warning signs" of what is yet to come.

FIRESTORMS

A firestorm is a blaze so hot and intense that it not only reduces physical matter to ash but it also literally eats up the atmosphere. Bye bye oxygen, bye bye life. Every so often we have a massive blaze in a forest somewhere that can level tens of thousands of acres, destroy homes, and kill wildlife and a few humans who didn't get out of the way fast enough. The recent massive blazes in New Mexico and Colorado are prime examples. A firestorm does not always happen, but it can. Here again, let's play the "what if" game.

Should a nuclear exchange occur, the resultant firestorm could well be its most destructive feature. But it would not necessarily take a nuclear war to fry the planet. If the massive atmospheric storms predicted by some "pole shifters" were to occur globally, lightning alone could set enough fires to toast us all (or at least suffocate us all) in massive firestorms.

And then we have our sworn mortal enemies in al-Quida. Nice folk. It is known that as I write this they are seriously working on plans to send out a hundred or so trained firebombers across our land. They would be "heavily armed" with a Bic lighter and perhaps a can or two of gasoline! Their mission? To torch hundreds of millions of acres of American forests and grasslands simultaneously. This would create firestorms so unimaginable that total victory over the infidels will be assured. What is scary about this plot is its minimal cost, its simplicity of execution and its real potential to destroy us as a nation.

Whether it be a massive super-volcano, a massive tsunami, a massive earthquake, a massive hurricane or a massive firestorm, the operative word is "massive". In theory any of these could occur at any time. They could occur tomorrow, next month, in December, or in a thousand years. Or never. The odds of any one of these actually happening on or around Decenber 21st are probably pretty low. But so were the odds of the USA Olympic hockey team beating the Russians or Ali beating Liston!

What if the Mayans were in fact given certain knowledge by an advanced civilization that 12/21/12 would be a very special day? What if these extraterrestrials could predict the future or cause an Apocalypse to happen on a pre-determined day at their whim? If so, then perhaps we should all enjoy every

day between now and December 21st to
the fullest!

PART SIX

<u>MAN-MADE APOCALYPSE</u>

"If an enemy wants to bring America to its knees, it will fire off an enormous electromagnetic pulse that erases every hard drive in the country. Within two weeks we'll all be wearing animal pelts and huddling in caves for warmth." Tom McNichol.

For a moment let's now all become Atheists (if you are not already), accept that there is no God to exact revenge on our pitiful species, and let's see what our fellow humans without any divine intervention could actually do to us all.

I read a scholarly article recently that postulated that if everyone who has a toilet flushed it at exactly the same time it would collapse the entire waste-water collection system countrywide and result in massive local flooding. I think the author was actually serious! Somehow I do not think a simultaneous poop-flush was what the Mayans were hinting! (Although this would certainly qualify as an Apocalypse for anyone who found themselves suddenly wallowing around ass deep in a lake full of crap.)

NUCLEAR STUFF

Today we have thousands of "weapons of mass destruction" that are beyond imagination. (Crappers are not one of them.) Comparatively, the "atom bombs" we dropped on Hiroshima and Nagasaki were kid's toys. Yet even their force was almost beyond human imagining. Hiroshima was an air-burst high above the surface, which minimized fallout. The Nagasaki blast on the other hand was a seriously dirty ground strike. Either way, Japan was devastated.

Aside note: What is seldom remembered is that the two atom bombs by themselves did NOT end Japanese involvement in WWII. It took many weeks of firebombing thereafter of the Japanese "wooden cities" to convince them that all was finally lost. They were one damn tough enemy.

Conventional WWII bombs, called blockbusters because they could devastate a city block, each held the equivalent destructive power of twenty tons of trinitrotoluene (TNT). Because of all the data available on conventional TNT, all bombs are rated in relation to their effective destructive power relative to a given amount of TNT.

If you were to add up the power of ALL the blockbusters dropped during ALL of WWII it equals some two-million tons, or "two megatons", of TNT.

The two bombs dropped on Japan were tiny by comparison to today's multi-megaton "Hydrogen Bombs", which have never been detonated except in tests. Never in anger. Yet. Had we developed hydrogen bombs before atom bombs there would be no Japan today! Multi-megatons in a single weapon, the equivalent of all the bombs dropped in WWII in the blink of an eye. Unimaginable.

A delightful chain of events happens in the vicinity of the detonation of a nuclear bomb. (And damn it, it is NOT pronounced "nook-**u**-lar"...think Sarah Palin and other powerful politicians who always mis-pronounce this very important word. It's "nook-**lee**-er" you dolts.) Also, any one with the remotest understanding of empirical scientific methodology also knows with 100% certainty that the earth is unimaginably older than a few thousand years, and that humans and scary old T. Rex did not ever cross paths. (Which was damn lucky for the early humans!)

I don't mean to disrespect any religion. There are four basic ways humans determine true from false. Intuition, favored by ancient philosophers and theologians, is the most highly subjective of these. It relies on inspiration, revelations, visions, dreams, imagination and guesswork. It has no basis whatsoever in reality.

Next we have truth imparted by authority figures. This is expert testimony from parents, teachers, friends, neighbors, clergy, politicians and celebrities, reinforced by endless repetition. This is the "knowledge" with which we grow up, and it becomes "common sense". There is no basis in fact, just hearsay.

Then there are the Rational Methods of determining truth. These are formal deductions based on things like mathematics, probability, analogies, interpolations, and statistics. These are more reliable than intuition or what someone tells you, but have many limitations.

Favored by all with scientific training, myself included, are the Empirical Methods of finding truth. This is the process of using careful observations and experiments to document a truth in a repeatable way by un-coerced investigators. When something, such as the speed of light or gravity, or the age of a rock or bone, is measured tens of thousands of times by thousands of scientists over a decades and they always get the same answer it gives one lots of confidence that a genuine truth has been found. The beauty of empirical science is that it is always being refined and improved upon to arrive at ever more reliable truths.

When we deal with Mayan calendar matters, the closest we can get to the truth is through rational methods. There are no possible empirical experiments to determine the truth. We know from empirical methods quite accurately what the result of various disaster scenarios would be. But to understand what may have inspired the Maya centuries ago to produce a series of calendars on stone tablets that seem to point to a certain date in time with some unknown meaning cannot be determined scientifically.

From empirical science, here is the chain of events Iran can expect if Israel decides to drop a few nukes over Tehran (or vice versa over Tel Aviv): The immediate effect is from the actual blast wave from each bomb. It simply flattens everything for a few miles around. Then there is the storm of gamma rays and neutrons that fry outlying humans from the inside out. And of course there is the oxygen-depleting firestorm. It would not take many such bombs to put Iran back into the stone age. Nor, for that matter, Israel, should Iran manage to bomb them first.

But what about a full-blown nuclear war, with the United States, Russia, China, North Korea, India and Pakistan and whoever else decides to join the party all popping off rocket after rocket tipped with "small" tactical a-bombs? Or maybe throw in a few hydrogen bombs just for the hell of it? There are seven billion people on earth. It is postulated that a full nuclear exchange of thousands of warheads would kill most all of them on the first day.

The few remaining survivors (for example, miners deep underground and submariners) would then be subjected to fatal surface radioactive fallout, which lasts a very long time. It takes almost a hundred years for the majority of the deadly Strontium 90 to disappear, longer for the even worse cesium 137. Fallout, however, may be the least of it.

No one can predict the climate effect of the huge radioactive cloud that would completely fill earth's skies in the event of a massive nuclear exchange. Global cooling, because the cloud reflects sunlight?   Global cooking from a "greenhouse effect"? No one knows for certain. Whichever, it is not good.

At the very least the nitrogen in the upper atmosphere will be burned into ozone-destroying oxides killing the protective ozone layer and admitting an immense dose of ultraviolet radiation. This radiation would kill almost anything left alive. The most likely survivors would be viruses! Those tough little buggers just might inherit what is left of the earth.

Of course, with so much potential for destruction, we keep a very tight rein on our nuclear stockpile, right? No possible room for error there. Sadly,not quite true. Not even close.

Are you aware that THREE hydrogen bombs have been dropped by accident into the water off the East Coast of the United States? This is a well-documented fact. Why has no effort ever been made to recover them? Surely if we can bring up dinner plates from Titanic we can retrieve a few dropped nukes, no?

Well, as far as I can tell, the reasoning is that these submerged nukes are "safe" as long as no one messes around with them! The ocean will simply eventually dissolve them. Whatever. Of course the government claims they pose absolutely no danger. Of course not. Nothing ever poses any danger. Just ask the government, who is always there to help and inform you. Not.

What is even more startling is that credible reports claim that ninety-two (92!) nuclear warheads, or much larger entire bombs, have been lost worldwide in military "mishaps" by both the USA and Russia. Fewer than half were ever recovered! In addition to those few mentioned above off the New Jersey coast there are around forty-three (43!) others just waiting to dissolve. Or explode. Or whatever. Chilling.

Our government claims that "only" eleven of ours' have not been recovered. That surely is very comforting to know. Are you comforted? I'm not.

What does all this have to do with 12/21/12? Nothing directly. It is simply an example of something rather important that has more or less been swept under the rug, "government whitewashed" if you choose to use that phrase. Forgotten? Whitewash 2012? 2012 Kablooie? What do "they" know that we do not?

Of course of even far greater immediate importance is the "small" matter of the thirty or so Russian "suitcase nukes" that were reported to be unaccounted for after the breakup of the Soviet Union. Each one is capable of totally destroying most of a large city.

As far as I can determine these small but deadly nuclear bombs are still missing and unaccounted for. Could they each be sitting in a storage locker in a major American city just waiting for a remote detonation signal? Maybe on 12/21/12? Who knows? And if "they" knew beforehand, would we ever be told? Unlikely.

Could the scenario postulated in Nelson De Mille's great book *"Wild Fire"* actually happen? He wrote this fictional but possible account about wealthy and secretive radical right-wing nut-jobs fiercely loyal to the USA. Their aim was to set off a few "purchased" suitcase nukes in two major American cities. The idea is that we would immediately assume the deed was perpetrated by Islamic radicals.

In retaliation we would immediately launch a nuclear attack against every country with a predominantly Muslim population! If you happen to be wearing a white robe or a burka you would be instant toast. That way any future threat from extremist Muslims would be gone forever. And so are a billion or so innocent people! What's left of the United States after the two sacrificial cities are nuked will be safe from Islamic extremists forever. Collateral damage?

Entirely acceptable. Interesting
scenario.

Let's give some thought first to Iran. It is
no secret that Mahmoud Ahmadinejad
(in Persian: Mahmūd Ahmadinezhād) is
known to be a zealous, truly believing,
deeply dedicated "twelver". He may be
a madman, or he may be totally rational,
it's all in the viewpoint. (Is there such a
thing as a rational madman?)

Either way MA has said openly that the
total annihilation of Israel (The Little
Satan) and the total annihilation of the
United States (The Great Satan) can
lead to the eventual appearance of the
beloved Mahdi, the Twelfth Imam.

He believes as deeply as you or I can
believe anything in our own religion that
we must have a world-wide Apocalypse
in order for this "Twelfth Imam" to
appear and unite Islam in an ultimate
worldwide Caliphate. I assume he

reasons that there will be something left for the Mahdi to unite!

Never forget the immortal words of Osama bin Laden: "The difference between we Islamists and you Westerners is that you love life and we love death."   So here we have a rather large group of zealots who actually want to die in the process of killing off everyone else. Novel concept. The scary thing is they're totally serious. And no amount of economic sanctions nor rhetoric nor "good-will" negotiations will ever change this.

Whether or not Iran has developed a functional nuclear bomb is irrelevant. There are recent reports that it has enough highly-enriched uranium on hand to fabricate five bombs (two for Israel and three for Uncle Sam?). North Korea and Pakistan, not exactly our loyal buddies, both do have a documented nuclear arsenal. It would be very simple for either of them to slip a few nukes into Iran if they thought that somehow it was in their best interest. As far as I'm concerned, Iran already has a nuke, probably supplied by either China or North Korea.

Now let's think as a madman with a mission and a dark sense of humor might think. With the whole world anticipating the possibility of some cataclysm on the Mayan-indicated December 21, 2012, why not choose that very special date to begin to set up the Mahdi's return and unleash nuclear mutual annihilation? Sounds to me like as good a day as any. Black humor? "You expect a catastrophe, check this one out world!". The joke's on you, Jay Leno!

None of this could ever happen you say? We humans are not THAT crazy? The threat of Mutually Assured Destruction, "M A D", will surely win the day. Well, think about the "Cuban Missile Crisis". We came damn close then, but MAD fortunately won the day. JFK had grapefruits. NK had grapes. Who has the biggest cahones this time around?

Now think about the Apocalypse that is "absolutely necessary" for the twelfth Mahdi to appear. M A D becomes the means, not the deterrent. Again, never forget the immortal words of the late Osama bin Laden, which I'll repeat: "The big difference between we Islamists and you Westerners is that you love life and we love death".   Martyrdom over living. That is one damn tough enemy to defeat!

As if Iran vs Israel & the USA isn't enough of a worry, we have North Korea (more useless talks and sanctions) vs South Korea, always good for a nuke or two. In fact, if North Korea can mooch an ICBM from China I'd think even

Honolulu might see a repeat of "Pearl Harbor" in spades!

And of course fully nuclear armed India and Pakistan, who truly hate each other, could "accidentally" put the whole planet at risk if one or the other decides to settle some old score over the Vail of Kashmir's sovereignty or whatever other hatred they can conceive. All these scenarios are rather disquieting to say the least.

Are there other exotic man made weapons that could cause serious consequences? Are we developing any? Are the Chinese? How about this disturbing little note: On April 15, 2012 it was reported that Russian President Vladimir Putin confirmed that his country is working on the creation of an electromagnetic gun that attacks its target's central nervous system, putting them in a zombie-like state.

According to Russian defense minister Anatoly Serdyukov, "When it was used for dispersing a crowd and it was focused on a man, his body temperature went up immediately as if he was thrown into a frying pan." It can fry your brain from the inside out! Wow! Let's figure out how to do this from a satellite or a drone before they do! Fun weapon.

VERY UGLY CYBER STUFF

How about an Apocalypse brought about not by a weapon but by a tiny button? That would be the "Enter" button on a computer, and we are talking here about cyber-attack. This is most certainly very possible. It actually happens daily on a less-than-apocalyptic level . Properly executed such an attack could take out our entire power grid, much as the Y2K bug threatened to do. Coronal mass ejections aside, in my opinion this is the single greatest threat we face today from which we could protect ourselves.

The roots of the cyber-security problem are the ubiquitous SCADA systems. SCADA stands for "Supervisory Control And Data Acquisition". These cyber-controls are used literally everywhere in modern society to control everything. They have replaced humans in tasks that were once dependably performed manually. Such mundane tasks as opening and closing valves in power plants and on pipelines and in chemical plants and refineries are now 100% SCADA controlled. If a hacker gets control, which is **very** far from impossible, worldwide power grids can be shut down. Pipelines could be destroyed. Deadly chemicals could be poured endlessly into the environment.

No less a figure than the highly-respected Richard Clark, a presidential adviser on cyber-security said: "They could cause power blackouts, not just by shutting off power but by permanently damaging generators that would take months to replace. They could do things like cause pipelines to explode. They could ground aircraft." "Sophisticated cyber-attacks could do things like derail trains across the country."

Clark continues to point out: "The US Military ran headlong into the cyber age, and we became very dependent on cyber devices without thinking it through. Without thinking that if someone got control of our software, what would we be able to do? Do we have backup systems? Can we go back to the old days".   Clearly the answer is **NO**. The fact is that American armed forces are vulnerable throughout, including command and control, supplies, as well as weapons systems".

CIA chief Leon Panetta recently stated: "The next Pearl Harbor could be a cyber attack". The Security & Defense Agenda, a Brussels defense think-tank, recently conducted a study of the world's top cyber-security experts. The results, released on January 30, 2012, showed that the majority believe that a global arms race is **already** taking place in cyberspace.

Many believe that cyber security is more important than either border security or even missile defense! Sadly, it was reported that the United States lags far behind most other developed nations in its preparedness for dealing with a cyber-attack.

There was a press conference on April 30th during the visit of Japan's Prime Minister Yoshihiko Noda to the United States. A question was asked of both he and President Obama relating to the upcoming first anniversary of the assassination of Osama bin Laden. President Obama responded with an assessment of whether a predecessor or future president would have given the kill order.

In contrast Prime Minister Nodo not only pointed out that the war on terrorism is far from over, but he also mentioned the real threat of CYBER ATTACK! When was the last time you heard any world leader talk about that as being a present terrorism concern? Is anyone listening? I sure hope so, because the threat is a very real and a very present danger.

Has an important international cyber-attack actually already happened? A couple of years ago either Israel or the United States or both in concert launched a cyber-attack against Iran's nuclear capabilities. It is reported to have set Iran's nuclear program back many years, by crippling a number of their key uranium-enrichment centrifuges. It was accomplished by way of a software program called Stuxnet, which we will discuss further below.

As recently as April 2012 an under-reported cyber-attack screwed up Iran's oil production facility. Curious. I wonder who pulled that one off. As I write this report, a major cyber-attack is reportedly underway aimed squarely at computer networks belonging to America's natural-gas pipeline companies. It threatens to shut down that vital industry in a heartbeat.

The Genesis of the entire cyber-attack problem lies in the fact that software programs were most often written by non-professional-developers, engineer/programmers, with zero expertise in cyber defense. Ralph Langner, a German security consultant, is quoted as saying: "At some point they learned how to develop software, but you cannot compare them to professional software developers who probably spent a decade learning."

A serious on-going worry is the above mentioned Stuxnet worm, used to attack Iran's Natanz nuclear facility. It is a massive piece of software, containing 15,000 lines of code! Langner points out that: "The attack vectors and exploits used by Stuxnet can be copied and re-used reliably against completely different targets. Until a year ago no one was aware of such an aggressive and sophisticated threat. With Stuxnet that has changed. It is on the table. The technology is out there on the internet". Scary stuff.

He goes on to point out that the West is disproportionately vulnerable because of its far greater dependence on the internet. Where militarily powerful western countries historically held a huge edge because of their advanced technologies, it is the vary lack of such advanced technology in developing countries that makes them almost immune to cyber-attack or counter-attack!

But as massive as the Stuxnet program is, it is dwarfed by "worm.Win32.flame", known simply as "Flame". Flame contains codes twenty-times as long! Vitaly Kamluk, chief malware expert at Russia's Kaspersky Labs cyber-security firm, pointed out that Flame is designed not to cause damage but to steal sensitive information.

"Once a system is infected, Flame begins a complex set of operations, including sniffing the network traffic, taking screenshots, recording audio conversations, intercepting the keyboard, and so on." says Kamluk.

Professor Alan Woodward of the Department of Computing at the University of Surry told the BBC: "This [Flame] is basically an industrial vacuum cleaner for sensitive information. Whereas Stuxnet just had one purpose in life, Flame is a tool-kit, so they can go after just about everything they can get their hands on".

Time.com reported on May 29th that the Flame program ".....surged through computers at the [Iranian] Ministry of Oil, wiping out hard drives and crashing several websites. One by one, oil terminals in the Persian Gulf were disconnected from the Internet to prevent further damage and a crisis committee was formed to deal with the fallout.

By the time the virus had been contained some 24 hours later, computers and websites from the National Iranian Oil Company, the

National Gas Company, the Ministry of Oil and several subsidiary companies had taken a hit, according to reports in the Iranian media."

Here is what is REALLY scary about Flame. Unlike Stuxnet, which was a super- sophisticated program probably created by a nation-state with vast technical resources, Flame is written mostly in "Lua". What is Lua? It's the programming used to create XBox games, and stuff like "Angry Birds"! Every computer geek on the planet can manipulate it as ever might fit their intentions.

It has been reported that the creators of Stuxnet (and a similar program called Duqu) and Flame apparently collaborated at some point in time. This conclusion was drawn by noting that an odd section of code called "Resource 207" appears in both programs.

Cyber threats come in five different flavors. Botnets are networks of geographically dispersed infected computers. These are remotely controlled to attack other computers and networks. DDOS (Distributed Denial Of Service) attacks crash websites by overwhelming them with fake traffic. Trojan Horses are extremely-common software programs that seem innocent, appearing to be something else. They can even be disguised as anti-virus software!

Best known, of course, are Viruses. There are more of them than any other threat because they are easy to create and distribute. They can be designed to make a computer or network malfunction in a variety of ways. Lastly, there are Worms. These are self-replicating viruses that can consume the entire memory on a hard drive.

"Malware" is a generic term covering all of the above.

There are three basic sources of malware. First, we have individuals, known as "hacktivists", who do it for the fun and challenge. They are essentially mischief-making geeks. "I'm a better hacker than you are!" is a common motivator for these brilliant morons. These folk can easily re-work Flame. Then there are the "cyber-criminals", whose sole intention is to steal something, money, data, information or whatever, for personal monetary gain. Flame is right up their alley.

Lastly, there are the Nation States with their massive available funding who create cyber-weapons. Stuxnet is likely one such program, far beyond the capabilities of a single hacktivist or even a private group of cyber criminals.

In case you were nodding off on this one, al Queda announced in mid-May (just before the Flame event!) that they were calling for a cyber-jihad, a cyber holy war, to be carried out against America. It would be aimed at our infrastructure, notably the electric grid. Launch date: December 21st?

An editorial ran recently in the conservative Iranian daily Kayhan. The editor is a very close associate of Supreme Leader Khamenei. It boasted that: "Skilled players have appeared who can, in a short period of time, do astonishing and unbelievable damage to American infrastructure. All they need is a connected computer and knowledge that is no longer under the exclusive control of Western countries." We had better prepare to be astonished. As of today we are simply not prepared to defend. It just might not have been an idle boast.

The United States definitely does possess an offensive cyber-attack capability. What we shockingly do NOT possess, according to *Smithsonian* magazine, "is any reliable proven defense capability against a cyber-attack." That is one act we'd better get together in a damn big hurry.

Congress is actually reported to be in the process of debating whether to grant the federal government the authority to require vital sectors, such as electric utilities, telephone companies, oil and gas companies and refineries, and chemical industries to meet certain levels of cyber security. The key word is "debating". Will anything useful come of these discussions? Let's hope so.

Of course it remains to be seen how this would all be paid for. Tax the top 1%? I think not. Cut wasteful spending and foreign aid to countries that hate us? Unthinkable! Let's just raise the debt limit and sell more bonds to China. What's another trillion or two?

Our entire utility grid, dependent 100% on computerized controls, could in theory be shut down entirely by some uber-brilliant 15-year-old propeller-head (Brooklyn slang for a geek wearing a beanie with a prop-on-top) working in his father's garage in Estonia! Beyond a doubt both China and Russia possess the capability. So probably does Iran. How's December 21st as the perfect date to try it out? Scary thought.

How important is the internet these days? I'm not certain we could exist for a week without it. Surely a cyber-attack could shut it down rather easily. In fact, on July 9, 2012, a worldwide cyber-attack-by-malware was reported to be a certainty. If your computer happend to be infected with the Trojan Horse malware called "DNS Changer", it was unable to correctly access the internet.

The date 07/09/12 was dubbed "Internet Doomsday". Apparently thousands of individuals' computers worldwide were infected without their knowledge. Even a good anti-malware program designed to counter similar infections may not have worked. The FBI was been long involved in obviating this problem, so you can believe it was taken very seriously.

But aside from a virus or a cyber-attack, a Presidential Executive Order, in the event of a real, contrived or imagined "National Emergency", could also totally shut off internet access. This seems possible, if not probable, in early December in advance of the 21st. After all, allowing us free access to news about the coming Apocalypse and thereby possibly creating panic just would not be in our best interest. Would it? Actually, maybe not.

Is it possible that we could accidentally annihilate ourselves? I have read reports of the immense concern top-level scientists had prior to the very first atomic bomb detonation test in the '40s. No one had a clue what might happen. Some postulated total global annihilation from some unanticipated atmospheric side- effect.   A collective sigh of relief was all that actually happened. Who knows what potentially earth-destroying experiments are being conducted worldwide? For example:

GERM WARFARE

If we do not have enough to worry about from all of the above, there is always the ever-present danger of "germ warfare". This very real danger does not get a lot of press coverage. Attempted widespread distribution of anthrax, or smallpox or SARS has been a reported concern for decades. Aside from the "mysterious white powder" which turns up occasionally in an envelope or box somewhere, we never hear of an impending "anthrax attack". As far as I can recall these anthrax scares always turn out to be pranks, using talcum powder or detergent powder as the "deadly white stuff".

Unfortunately there are far worse possible infections than anthrax. Ebola is, of course, one of these. Having your body dissolve from the inside out seems like a very ugly way to die. Fortunately, no one to date has figured out how to isolate and spread this nasty stuff. Just don't get bitten by an infected monkey!

The good news (term used lightly) is that the problem with mounting a germ warfare attack has always been the difficult one of finding a reliable way to infect a large and targeted population. Do you attack the water supply? Do you infect some common food item, like BigMacs? Can you find a reliable airborne infector? Just what "germ" will reliably kill the most people the fastest?

Believe it or not there are laboratories all over the world working feverishly to develop "super bugs" this very day. If they can take a very lethal existing bug that selectively infects, say, chickens by direct contact, and find a way to create mutations of it so that it spreads through the air and kills humans, they have accomplished their "goal". Whoopee! Well guess what? They have recently accomplished their goal!

Two laboratories, working in cooperation with each other, one in Wyoming, U.S.A., and one in The Netherlands, have figured out how to take the H5N1 bird flu virus (lethal to birds and only transmitted by direct contact) and mutate it together with H1N1 swine flu virus, so that the new super-bug is both lethal to humans **and** transmittable through the air! The June 2, 2012 issue of Science News reports in great detail about this latest attempt to play God and create new life. The first announcement of this potential pandemic mutation was made by the Dutch at a conference in Malta in late 2011.

America's governing authority over such matters is the National Science Advisory Board for Biosecurity (NSABB). (Ever hear of them? Not exactly a household acronym.) It is reported that initially the Board: ".....decided that open publication posed too great a risk of misuse, recommending the publication of severely redacted versions". "At the end of March, the Board reversed its decision, ruling....that the benefits of information sharing outweighed the risks." Are these people totally crazy? Do we actually pay these people for doing this crap?

To my mind this smacks of treason. This was in direct opposition and contradiction to the British Royal Board conclusion: "The Board found that these results had an unusually high magnitude of risk." Duh.

We are simply talking about the very lives of every American citizen! Are we asking for a pandemic? Where is the public outcry? Where is the media coverage? Where is our President whose primary responsibility is protecting Americans from harm? Where is Mitt Romney? They are all AWOL on this one!

Here is the really scary part. The scientific papers, the "cookbooks" with easy-to-follow directions for creating this ugly super-bug, were initially marked "NOT FOR PUBLICATION". But in their infinite wisdom our good old reliable NSABB made the decision to publish the results so that every terrorist on the planet has certain knowledge of how to kill us all. The Dutch actually published the entire paper in Nature 05/02/12. Incredible but true. Media coverage? Zero. Outrage? None. Why? You guess.

Every Iranian biochemist is salivating! Can you imagine the panic that could spread if even a rumor of the release, accidental or otherwise, of this killer mutated super-bug hit the social media around December 21st? And what if it were not a rumor? 2012 Kablooie!

OTHER STUFF

Getting back to "accidental annihilation" scenario, let's take a quick look at today's massive "super-colliders". Scientists shoot various tiny sub-atomic particles at each other at unimaginable speeds by way a huge multi-mile long circular tube to see what happens when they collide.

The even smaller particles that result are categorized into a grand theory of particle physics, the answer to "What Is Everything Made Of". They think they have found all but one particle, the elusive Higg's Boson, and perhaps even evidence of its existence. But that is not the point.

There are some high-up in the scientific community who seriously believe that these well-meaning scientists could inadvertently create a "black hole", and that such an entity could somehow grow and eventually destroy the planet! Of course those in control of the Supercollider laugh at this possibility. Ha, ha.

Far more likely, a real and present danger, is the unleashing by some ruling nut-job of a chemical weapon. Russia in particular is reported to have enough toxins stored up to kill a hundred billion people, about fourteen times earth's entire population! Not even a cat has enough lives to survive such an attack!

Some really nasty stuff, like plague or Ebola actually exists in petri dishes in many bio-labs around the world. It is not hard to imagine some madman finding a way to put get this stuff airborne and injecting enough of it into the atmosphere to kill virtually everyone. We live in very dangerous times on a very fragile pebble in space, dubbed by Carl Sagan: "A Pale Blue Dot". We can easily become pale white humans.

Lastly, we could always face the complete breakdown of civilized society through riots and looting and killing. It is not hard to imagine the total collapse of the monetary system worldwide. We are much closer to that than any government will ever admit. This could lead to massive food shortages and riots beyond imagining.

Equally frightening is the possibility of massive civil unrest after the November election if enough citizens believe the election was blatantly stolen somehow by the "wrong side". Ever give thought to the incredible fact that our electronic voting machines are now all owned and provided by a Spanish consortium run by Europeans? How the hell did that come to pass?

Any electronic machine can be rigged. Think Vegas "slot machines" which can be set to return **any** percentage of bets the "house" decides on. Could not an electronic voting machine be set to "flip" every third vote from candidate A to candidate B?

Could not outsiders, even without the knowledge of the candidate of their choice, pay huge sums of money to some programmer to rig the voting machines in favor of his chosen candidate? Could there even be a bidding war to pay the programmer the most money to rig the machines one way or the other? This could be an interesting election!

Massive civil unrest can surely lead to Martial Law. Is this being anticipated? Is that what all of those reported empty huge detention centers around the country are waiting for? What about the nationwide fleet of spy-drones I keep reading about? Any possible connection here? Just asking.

If December 21st is not "The End Of Time" but is actually simply a "New Beginning" as some interpret the long-count Mayan calendar's end as indicating, there is certainly no assurance that such a new beginning will be a beginning we would care to face.

PART SEVEN

<u>EXTRATERRESTRIALS</u>

"There is no danger that the Titanic will sink. The boat is unsinkable, and nothing but inconvenience will be suffered by the passengers." Philip Franklin, V.P., White Star Lines, after learning that Titanic had hit an iceberg.

DATELINE NOVEMBER 2011, WHITE HOUSE, WASHINGTON D. C.: "The U. S. Government has no evidence that any life exists outside our planet, or that an extraterrestrial presence has contacted or engaged any member of the human race. In addition, there is no credible information to suggest that any evidence is being hidden from the public's eye."

How about "non-credible" evidence? Are you reassured? I most certainly am not. They go on to acknowledge that the very existence of alien life is probable, but that the vast distances throughout the Cosmos make contact with humans highly unlikely. But not impossible.

I have heard it said that only morons, the naïve, and the uneducated believe in UFOs and extraterrestrials. I've been called all of these and worse. I can assure you I am none of the above. And I do believe in intelligent life beyond earth. (I'm not entirely certain I believe in intelligent life **ON** earth!)

When I was thirty-one (seems like only yesterday!) I read Erich von Daniken's startling new book "*Chariots Of The Gods*". Thereafter, I was a true dedicated believer in extraterrestrials . His reasoning made a lot of sense to me then, and still does. Since then he has written a mere thirty-one books and is credited with selling sixty-three million copies overall! A lot of people obviously do give a damn! In his more recent

2010 "*Twilight of the Gods*" he predicts the return to earth once again of these extraterrestrials. I do not doubt it for an instant.

In Shakespeare's Hamlet, Act III, Scene II, he penned the phrase: "Methinks the Lady protesteth too much". It referred to a torrent of contrary- statements that were clearly made for the purpose of hiding an actual truth. And thus it appears to be with the White House and NASA and JPL and everything else that comes out of our government with regard to what might or might not happen on December 21st. They just continue to protest too much the possibility that we should look at December 21, 2012 as having any possible special significance.

The classic case in point of government denial is of course "Area 51". Weather balloon? Really? Recently, on May 3, 2012 an event occurred that to me is equally suspicious. "Whitewash 2012"? My son Bert pointed out to me an article so under-reported that I missed it completely. It relates to a recent live streaming video from the "Solar and Heliospheric Observatory" known as SOHO. This is a satellite launched in 1995 as a joint NASA/European Space Agency venture specifically to study our sun and its activities.

On two recent occasions, the latest on last May 3rd, the SOHO video images appeared to show a mysterious, huge, rectangular object in the immediate vicinity of the sun! This rather fuzzy image is, of course, subject to viewer interpretation. The image certainly shows "something" there. As soon as this object was noticed and reported, NASA suspiciously disabled the video stream immediately, never to be seen again. Talk about food for conspiracy theorists!

The mysterious "something" of course was immediately explained away by Washington as either a natural phenomenon, or a glitch in the imaging system. The do, in fact, protesteth too much. How about an alien spacecraft waiting to pounce on December 21st? Aliens? Extraterrestrials? Just asking.

Back in the '90s some woman famously claimed that she had an implant put in her brain by aliens, and that she was chosen by these aliens to warn earth of a coming collision-catastrophe in 2003. I guess I was out of town when it happened! Anyway, she has now revised the date to, of all dates, 12/21/12. What a surprise! Truly amazing coincidence.

If you accuse me of being a devoted Star Trek fan I'd gladly say: "Guilty as charged!" I have been a science fiction enthusiast since I was a child. I haven't read everything ever written by Isaac

Asimov, but I've tried! A fellow MENSAN, I believe he is credited with writing over six-hundred sci-fi books and short stories. Though less prolific as writers, the late Ray Bradbury and Robert Heinlein are my other favorites. Really great reads.

Movies such as "*2001 – A Space Odyssey*", "*Avatar*", and "*John Carter*", along with the "*Star Wars*" and "*Star Trek*" series, as well as the three "*Men In Black*" movies, have always captured my imagination.

Recently I saw "*Prometheus*" in 3D, and was blown away by its sheer beauty, not to mention its basic premise. Was human life on earth seeded by an alien race? Quite likely. But one thing struck me as fascinating. Director Ridley Scott chose a very interesting date for the future landing on an alien world. It was briefly shown on-screen as **December 21st** albeit seventy years or so in the future! Apparently Mr. Scott is an Apocalypse 2012 non-believer, and wanted to make that point clear! It is interesting to see the date is actually on his radar screen.

I bought my first telescope when I was ten. I had saved up for it for a year. It was called a "SkyScope", a 3½" Newtonian Reflector, state of the art for amateur scopes in the mid '40s. I still proudly own it! Today I have my own large automated domed observatory which, together with its fully-automated large aperture catadioptric scope cost me more than would a loaded Mercedes! I am truly an "astronomy nut".

The death of Carl Sagan affected me more than most of my family passings. His "Cosmos" TV series, and book, should be required viewing and study by everyone before they are ever granted a high school diploma. There was one point he made almost in passing that impressed me more than anything I have ever contemplated. He stated that there are more stars in the cosmos than there are grains of sand on all of the beaches on earth. That's one hell of a lot of stars!

Each galaxy contains hundreds of billions, if not trillions of stars. Our own Milky Way Galaxy, a rather medium sized unremarkable galaxy, is said to contain around a half-trillion stars itself. These numbers are quite beyond any human understanding. That is one point I hope to make in this chapter. We simply cannot comprehend numbers this big.

A multi-year study conducted by astronomers at the European Southern Observatory (ESO) was published May 23, 2012 in Astronomy and Astrophysics journal. They concluded that there are tens of billions of rocky planets within the "Goldilocks Zone" (not too hot, not too cold, just the right temp) around stars in our own home Milky Way galaxy! These planets can have liquid water, and thus can sustain life as we know it. Earth-like planets are very, very far from being unique.

The comprehension of numbers this large are beyond the grasp of even mathematicians or physicists or astronomers. Each of us has a different level of numeracy, the grasp, the "feel", of numbers. The following two stories may help to illustrate this point. They show the wide disparity between the understandings of numbers among different individuals.

There were two aristocrats out riding one day when one challenged the other to a contest. "Let's see who can come up with the largest number", suggested the first. "Great idea!", said the second. There was a pause of a few minutes when one finally shouted out: "Three!". There was an even longer pause, when, after deep thought, the other simply shrugged his shoulders and conceded defeat!

Then there is the story of a mathematician who was visiting a sick friend, also a mathematician, in the hospital. He had come by taxi, and casually remarked, trying to make small talk, that he had arrived in a taxi with the very boring serial number of 1729.

"No, no", excitedly exclaimed his ill friend. "That is a wonderful number! I can see clearly that it is the smallest possible number that is the sum of two cubes in two different ways! (For the record, nine cubed plus ten cubed, and one cubed plus twelve cubed both equal 1,729.)

Everyone's understanding of numbers falls somewhere between these two extremes, unfortunately more, I fear, towards that of the two aristocrats! Personally, I try to relate very large numbers to something familiar that I can visualize, such as counting off seconds, or laying one-dollar bills end to end.

Understanding large numbers is not only relevant to grasping the possible existence of extraterrestrials because of the immense number of stars. It is also relevant when pondering the United States' crushing direct national debt. It is presently over fifteen TRILLION dollars. By some accounts, if one considers every one of America's future obligations, the sum is over SIXTY trillion. And we seem eager and ready to add a mere trillion or so periodically just for the fun of it.

Our "official" National Debt actually stands at about sixteen-trillion dollars as I write this. It grows by three-million dollars a minute! USA Today reported that the United States government owes $61.6 TRILLION in unfunded obligations. These numbers are truly beyond comprehension, just as are the number of planets in our galaxy. Our American debt approaches the total Gross National Product of all of the nations on the entire planet!

The American Public at large cannot begin to grasp the enormity of this financial problem, and the politicians seem equally incapable of addressing it in any meaningful way. Some economists believe that it cannot possibly BE addressed, and that a total world-wide monetary collapse is inevitable, and sooner than later. 2012 Kablooie?

We are fiscally irresponsible to an extent that very few can begin to grasp. So let's look at "grasping" large numbers:

Let's start by counting off seconds, one-one-thousand, two-one-thousand, three-one-thousand....... One can, with a little practice, learn the proper cadence, and count off many minutes with quite good accuracy this way. Try it; it's fun! If we were to count to one thousand this way it would take about seventeen minutes.

Ten thousand seconds would take us just under three hours, and tax our patience to the limit! But how about a hundred thousand seconds? Well, that would take us a bit over three whole nine-hour working days! And now we get into some really big numbers. How about counting to one million? Here we are talking about counting for two working months, nine hours a day, every day. We'd be in a padded cell by then!

What about a thousand times that many, a billion seconds? Million, billion, no big deal. Let's forget about sleep, let's just count for twenty-four hours a day, day in and day out. It would take thirty-two years! If you started around 1980 you would just be finishing up. A billion is surely a big number. But what about a trillion? That's thousand billion, or a thousand thousand million. It's just a single letter different, a billion, a trillion, so what's the big deal?

Remember, the National Debt is fifteen trillion dollars. There are trillions of stars, and most we now believe, surrounded by trillions of planets. A trillion anything is a lot of it!

Well, it would take a person, counting at one-second intervals, ever since 30,000 BC, a mere thirty-two millennia ago to reach one single trillion!!! What was going on back then? Neanderthals were roaming through Europe! I doubt whether they could count at all. And what is the United States national debt?

That's fifteen trillion dollars folks, one damn big number. You would have begun counting your seconds off in 450,000 BC!

Not surprised or impressed? Let's look at these big numbers a different more physical way, seeing how long a line one could make laying United States currency bills end to end. Each bill is a tiny 6.14 inches long. You could jump across the five or so feet of ten bills laid end to end.

Lay a hundred end to end and it would take two Olympic long-jumps to cover the fifty-one feet. One thousand bills would stretch out almost two football fields. Ten-thousand bills would stretch a mile, about a ten minute walk or a one-minute drive.

One-hundred-thousand bills would stretch for ten miles, about a ten minute drive. But how about a million bills?

Laid end to end, a million bills would stretch for a hundred miles, about a two hour drive! A billion bills? Just an "m" to a "b". These would circle the entire planet earth four times!!   That's a big difference for simply exchanging a "b" for an "m".

But these days we hear "trillions of dollars" spoken of like it's no big deal. A trillion dollars?   Laid end to end, a trillion bills would reach from the earth to the sun, some ninety-three million miles!!! It takes light itself about seven minutes to traverse that distance. A trillion is a really, really big number.

Sixteen trillion is a really, really, REALLY big number! In dollars, that's our present National Debt! That's over seven round trips from the earth to the sun in end-to-end bills! It would take light itself traveling at 186,000 miles/second over an hour and a half to whiz by our National Debt in fifteen-trillion one-dollar bills laid end to end! We are really screwed.

Big Numbers can actually be fun to play with. There is a little party game that many find astounding.   If I asked you to give me a penny today, and twice as much tomorrow, two cents, and continue to double the amount you gave me every day for a 31-day month (one cent, two cents, four cents, etc.), take a quick guess of how much you would be giving me on the last day.

Did you guess a hundred dollars? A thousand dollars? Ten-thousand dollars?   No, that would be at the end of three weeks. Did you guess a hundred-thousand dollars? Few ever guess that high.   Heck, we started with a just penny three weeks ago. Not even close!

How about a million dollars? That would come at the end of four weeks. But on the 31st day you would pay me over ten-million dollars!! The total number is $10,798,243. Seriously! Numbers are weird! Most people have not a clue.

The brilliant visionary writer Arthur C. Clarke said: "Innumeracy is an even greater danger than illiteracy." Once we started teaching social and environmental awareness to the exclusion of fundamental math and language skills, we as a country began our downward spiral compared to other developed countries in both academic areas. We are, in the words of Tucson AM drive-time radio announcer John Justice, on "an endless parade of stupid"!

Professional astronomers are just beginning to find hundreds of planets orbiting stars in our Milky Way galaxy, which in itself, with its half-trillion stars, is a collection of those tiny sand grains of which Sagan so eloquently spoke. It appears that planets are the rule, not the exception.

That's a lot of planets, and that's in just our one of trillions of galaxies. The point is, we can be quite certain that the number of planets in all of the galaxies in the universe is a number so large that it in itself is beyond human comprehension, counting seconds and lining up dollar bills notwithstanding.

With so many planets, how can anyone possibly believe that we are alone? It is inconceivable. In "COSMOS" Carl Sagan, the greatest astronomy-communicator of all time, stated: "To me, it seems far more likely that the universe is brimming over with life."

Now let's look at time frames as if looking at a calendar. It has been pointed out that if one thinks of the life on planet earth in terms of a 365 day calendar, that civilization as we live it today has existed for only the last few minutes of December 31st! This is absolutely astonishing. My grandparents were born before electric lights, cars and airplanes. I was born before commercial television and jet airliners or microwave ovens! You were probably born before Blackberries and XBoxes!

So much progress in so little time. It is impossible to imagine what society will be like in a thousand, or ten thousand years or a million years. There could easily be civilizations out there many millions of years more advanced than are we. What wonders could their scientists have conceived in a million years, noting how much we have accomplished in one-ten-thousandth of that time? My grandma's family rode around in horse-drawn buggies and that's just a few generations ago. (At least the Amish have a choice!) The future possibilities boggle the mind.

There is absolutely no reason why some other planet somewhere out there could not be unimaginably more advanced than we are. If you are a Star Trek fan think of the "Q Continuum" and the great character "Q". I believe it is absolutely certain that omnipotent (by our standards) beings such as Q really do exist. Or the less-omnipotent but quite unusual Borg. As far as I am concerned, advanced beings have clearly visited us in the past, and will surely do so again.

Also, from the original Star Trek TV series, do you remember the "Squire Of Gothos", Trelaine? He was a seemingly- omnipotent being, and he turned out to be only a young child of his species playing with his human toys! He could be here in a flash. December 21st? Go ask a Mayan.

Ancient texts seem to have a common denominator. Many speak of artificial insemination by "Gods". Was Mary's immaculate conception caused in this manner? What about the immaculate conception of Noah? Ever hear of that one?

According to one of the recently transcribed Dead Sea Scrolls, Noah was the unfathered son of Lamech. Lamech was Methuselah's son and Enoch's grandson. It was Enoch who somehow had prior knowledge of the coming great flood, apparently having been given this prior knowledge by extraterrestrials (God?). This knowledge was passed on to Noah, who built the ark and saved all living creatures.

I do not believe for an instant that massive buildings such as those Mayan structures found in Mexico and points south could have been built by mere humans. As pointed out earlier, the

Mayans never even invented the wheel! I don't care how many of them pecked away at stones with other harder stones to make the building-stones flat and square, and smooth. Or for that matter how creative they were in moving multi-ton blocks and hoisting them into place and fitting them incredibly tightly together simply using massive amounts of slave-power.

That level of sophisticated construction just could not logically or possibly have been accomplished with human muscle and sweat alone. Least of all by the Mayans. The constructions at Puma Punka in the Bolivian Andes Mountains, and El Enladrillado in Chile are so incredibly huge and complex and perfect that it would be virtually impossible for humans **today** to construct them even by employing modern tools and machinery!

It is far easier to believe that vastly superior beings, extraterrestrials employing unimaginably advanced technology, lent the indigenous peoples a hand. A very big hand. In fact, these aliens were so good at construction that Mayan legend has it that one of their massive pyramids was built by extraterrestrials in a single day! Much of the pictographic "writing" the Mayans left behind is interpreted as clearly supporting the extraterrestrial-assistance hypothesis.

Do you recall the Twilight Zone episode when apparently-benevolent ready-to-please-humans extraterrestrials landed on earth? Their leader carried a book titled: "To Serve Man". They were eagerly welcomed with open arms. It turned out to be a cookbook! Such extraterrestrials need not even be sentient beings. They could well be robots or drones conceived by minds unimaginably more advanced than ours'.

In the past few years sightings of UFOs have increased very sharply. Of course, most are explained away by our government as natural phenomena of some sort, or outright hoaxes. This is the usual government whitewash. Think Roswell, New Mexico and "Area 51". Think the recent "object" mentioned earlier recently sighted near the sun. In truth, many UFOs have simply never been adequately explained.

Are we being watched? Are we being scouted for the mother-ship to come and wipe us all away? Or are the aliens already here, buried deep within the earth as depicted in *"War Of The Worlds"*? *Or are shape-shifters walking among us as depicted in "Men In Black"?* Beware the hidden middle third eye!

Were the Mayans, who I believe must have been visited by extraterrestrials, told the precise date these vastly-advanced beings would return to earth? Was that date December 21, 2012? We will soon know.

And let's hope they leave their cookbooks home!

PART EIGHT

<u>BE PREPARED</u>

"Undoubtedly, the desire for food has been, and still is, one of the main causes of great political events." Bertrand Russell.

"A hungry people listens not to reason, nor cares for justice." Seneca The Younger, Rome.

"I am always doing that which I cannot do, in order that I may learn how to do it". Pablo Picasso.

The term "survival" is relative. If we have an earth-shattering cataclysm, it will make absolutely no difference what preparations you make. In that event, we are all toast. Preparations, as with resistance to The Borg, are futile.

But what about a somewhat lesser event? By far the most likely scenario, on December 21st, or at any time in the future, is the total collapse of the electric power grid. Depending on exactly why it collapsed, solar storm, cyber-attack, or whatever, you could be looking at a week, a month, a year, decades or forever. You are faced with the decision of just how long you want to sustain the physical life of you and your family if such an event were actually ever to occur. And "occur" is extremely likely.

A very useful wake-up exercise is to stay at home for a week. Make no prior preparations, such as stocking up on water and food. Turn off your electric system at the source. Turn off your water supply main valve. No power, no water. Unplug your phone, and hide all portable communication devices. Unplug your computer. Of course if the power grid goes down you have no access to your money, or to communications, and you are limited to the gasoline in your car's tank.

Now see how long you can go before you realize just how serious this matter can be. Personally, I'm uncomfortable after the first hour when I can't check my email! Most are OK for a day. Day two gets testy. Few can go much longer without sensing something terribly wrong. By the end of a week, when all that is left to eat are cans of pet food, most are convinced of how much we rely on electricity for literally everything.

The past debacle with lack of government rapid-response to Hurricane Katrina is well documented though mostly forgotten. George Bush was blamed. What else is new. But at the end of this past June an event with even more widespread catastrophic effect hit much of the East Coast of the United States. A very rare weather phenomenon called a "derecho" killed two-dozen or so people and knocked out power for millions for a week or more.

A derecho can be thought of as a horizontal tornado. The word is a Spanish adverb meaning "straight". Technically it is a "bow echo" line of severe thunderstorms that travels horizontal to the ground in a straight line, just above the ground itself. This is the main distinction between a tornado and a derecho

My brother-in-law Jeff called me from Linwood, New Jersey and reported dozens of massive trees down, including a few on top of his car and house! Worst of all, residents were all told they would be without electrical power for at least a week! They went through this above-suggested Apocalypse exercise with no choice of starting date. No light, no air conditioning, no gasoline, no water. Not a great scenario to live through.

And where was FEMA this time around? Apparently AWOL, at least in southern New Jersey. And don't blame George Bush as with Katrina. The one fact that you **MUST** understand is that in a widespread emergency you are **ON YOUR OWN**. You simply cannot rely on any help from the government, which is not prepared for large-scale catastrophes. You must make preparations yourself **in advance** to protect your family from harm.

Do you need any more proof that the government cannot take care of you, no matter how many departments it creates to "save us from disasters"? It is in fact the government that is to blame, but **not** for weak responses to disaster. They **are** to blame for the **complacency** of our citizens.

It is the fault of the people themselves for not taking the necessary measures to care for themselves prior to **inevitable** disasters. <u>How many more lessons have to happen to drive this point home?</u> Once you cast off the shackles of complacency you will find out what freedom and liberty are really all about

So what should you stock up on for the short or long haul? Probably the most important item is water. You can live for an astonishingly long time on minimal rations, but only a few days without water. I'm not talking about a few five-gallon bottles. I'm talking about hundreds, if not thousands of gallons. There are many relatively-inexpensive polyethylene bulk tanks for sale. Buying one and filling it with potable water would not be a bad idea for starters.

For food, the simplest and most practical, and least expensive, are sacks of rice and sacks of beans. Also, a ton or so of canned goods will probably keep a year or more. If possible buy the kinds that open with a pull tab. You will still need a few good-quality manual can openers to open some cans. I assume they still make them. Perhaps try an antique store!

There are a number of companies that sell MREs (freeze-dried "meals ready to eat"). Some companies claim that these will last for 25 years! I'll have to make it to 100 to outlive their shelf-life! They are not cheap, but if a steady diet of rice and beans does not appeal to you stock up on a few year's supply of yummy MREs.

And don't forget pet food. Fido and Fluffy have to eat too! Unless you decide to eat them. According to President Obama, as the punch line of a Palin joke parody, and alluding to having eaten dog meat as a child: "Pitbulls are delicious"!

Of course if you hope to be able to cook anything or heat water, stock up on camp stoves and propane cylinders. Even Sterno-fired stoves will be fine, as long as you have stocked up on many cans of Sterno. And don't forget having a way to ignite them. You need to stock up on waterproof matches and butane lighters.

But here is your biggest problem. If we have a major, or even relatively-minor long-term power outage, there are going to be huge mobs of people who made no preparations whatsoever. They will be starving, they will be thirsty, they will be desperate, and they will probably be armed.

Are you prepared to defend your food and water storehouse? This part of the equation is missing from the above one-week simulation. Is protecting anything long-term even possible? Can you adequately hide your emergency supplies? These are the issues that you must contemplate and for which you must prepare.

One needs to look no further than the "Occupy" movement to get some idea what a crazed mob of anarchists looks like. And they're not even hungry! Multiply the Chicago mob from May or the later San Diego mobs by a hundred or so and….well, you get the idea. Not a pretty sight descending on your neighborhood or coming up your driveway. (Ever wonder who pays to support these Occupy people? Who pays for their travel and their meals? Just asking.)

And in case you do not believe that cannibalism would be impossible, think "The Donner Party". Think "*Soylent Green*". In an Apocalypse the unthinkable becomes the possible and even the probable.

For some level of defense, a 12 gauge shotgun and hundreds of rounds of ammunition is a good choice. So is an AK47 or AR15. I suspect that as we approach December 21st the sales of these weapons and associated ammunition will skyrocket. Being armed is a must. Supplies of weapons and ammo will become scarce.

In addition to food, there are a number of other items I consider absolutely essential for your survival in a mega-disaster. If you take medicines that sustain your health, you'd better have a year or more supply stashed away in a cool location.

Bottles of aspirin, naproxyn, and ibuprofen could be useful. And be certain to buy a supply of special iodine tablets for some thyroid protection in the event of radioactive fallout. See below for vendors.

Also, having liquid tincture of iodine and chlorine bleach on hand could help you purify your drinking water long-term. Of course it would be nice to have a large supply of toilet paper on hand too! How the Arabs do it with sand is beyond me!

Let's talk communication. Everyone should have an AM/FM/World-Band radio that runs either off solar power or via a hand crank. They are readily available, and quite inexpensive. Batteries do not last forever. In a disaster scenario, hopefully, someone somewhere will be broadcasting something useful. Then again, maybe not. Remember the movie "*On The Beach*". Human caused distress signal or rocking coke bottle? Scary stuff.

The ultimate would be for you to have a short-wave ham-radio station set up, also solar powered. In the event of an Apocalypse, ham radio operators on solar power may be the only real source of worldwide communication. This would be especially true if a major solar flare fries the communications satellites and cell phones become cute high-tech paperweights.

Having a number of flashlights and a large supply of batteries is not a bad idea. A better idea is to stock up on solar-powered garden lights. At around two bucks apiece they can put out a lot of light for a little money, and should last almost forever. Of course, you can always stock up on wax candles and matches.

Where you live will determine to some extent just how safe you might be. Living in a remote location is best if you can afford to do so. If a "great flood" for whatever reason seems possible, then the higher above sea level the better. If living remotely isn't practical for you, I'd certainly choose Hawaii over Detroit!

You can always consider going "underground". I can vividly recall back in the days of extreme nuclear paranoia there was a thriving industry in "bomb shelters". The government published booklets on how to make them yourself. I assume they still do.

Well, guess what? Survival shelters back! A number of companies are offering a wide range of "shelters for every occasion". Hardened Structures Company in Virginia Beach, Virginia, and Radius Engineering in Terrell, Texas, are leading the charge. Capitalism at its finest!

Not to be outdone, a California firm, Vivos has built an entire "survival community" in Indiana designed to house several hundreds of individuals. They are reported to be completing a second one in California as I write this. They do think of everything. Expensive as they are to get a ticket in to disaster-paradise, there is a growing waiting list of concerned Americans.

For those of you who can't afford the ten-grand or so for a place in solid-steel-city paradise, for a lesser amount you can assure that your bloodline endures even if you do not. You see, they also have an on-site cryogenic-vault where you can have your sperm and eggs frozen for later resuscitation. That is if there is anyone left around to make the wake-up call! You and Ted Williams.

In the event that some remnant of civilization remains, you will have to "buy" things you need that might (or likely might not) be available. A more accurate word is "barter". "Buy" implies money which you will either not have, or you will find to be of zero value.

Paper money, stocks, bonds and CDs will be totally worthless. So will your checking accounts! Without an electric grid none of these have value. There will BE no banking, no stock market, no bond market. Think in these terms: Whatever you consider to be of necessity for your own survival will likely be of equal necessity and value to others.

The best medium of exchange in my mind will be ammunition, in assorted calibers. .22, .25, .32, .357 and .45. Stock up on thousands of rounds of each. Vegetable seeds could also be useful for barter. So could cartons of cigarettes, and bottles of booze.

Don't forget matches and butane lighters. Even toilet paper! Barter will become the only way to obtain anything, short of armed theft. Sadly, the latter last resort will become commonplace.

Money, in the classical sense will be useless. Historically, precious metals have never been worth zero, as say the TV ads quite correctly. The smallest denomination precious-metal coins would possibly be of some use. United States dimes from the silver-era can be purchased in bulk bags, and would be a great choice.

If you want to stock up on some gold, stick to 1/10th, 1/20th or 1/25th, or 1/64th ounce coins. The smaller the unit of exchange the better.

Even if the "only" Apocalypse we suffer is the very likely collapse of the world-wide monetary system in the next few years you will be very happy that you stocked up on precious metals, whose value is predicted by many to skyrocket. There are many expert economists predicting the inevitability of the worldwide monetary collapse, sooner than later.

Worst case scenario? A world as depicted by Hollywood after a nuclear cataclysm?   In that event you might actually **want** to die, more quickly rather than slowly and painfully. Guns are reported to be good for that. So is a fast acting poison. You can check out the latter possibility out on the internet.

Do take family survival seriously. In the "best case scenario", you might not have to buy food again for a year or more.

And you'll have one hell of a lot of extra loose pocket change!

PART NINE

<u>LET THEM KNOW YOU KNOW</u>

"Truth has no special time of its own. Its hour is now …. always." Albert Sweitzer.

It is my fervent hope that after you have read this book you have developed some real concern about the various disasters that could strike on, before, or after December 21st. Whether or not the Mayan calendar-end portends anything, there is genuine potential for your life to be changed in terrible ways. For your own sake and for the sake of your loved ones (including Fido and Fluffy) you should be genuinely concerned.

I hope that you have decided to take preparedness actions. Don't panic, but the time to begin is NOW. Time is growing short, and December 21st is absolutely guaranteed to arrive on time! One or more of the earlier described disasters are virtually guaranteed to arrive at some time in your life.

I shared some ideas above on some key steps you can take at once. You probably have zero experience in making such preparations. Depending on your age, health, and circumstances, it may seem like a daunting task. I know you can do it once you set your mind to it and get started. Please do not hesitate.

One rather painless action you could take today would be to write letters to various government officials and key individuals. Writing such letters is a good first step for you to take. It might inspire the recipient to actually do something that could help you and your family and your neighbors survive in the long run. The responses you receive could at least provide you with a basis and direction toward being prepared.

To whom should you write? President Barack Obama, the Commander and Chief and leader of the free world would be a good place to start. I have yet, as of this writing, heard a single word from him about any possible apocalyptic dangers we face in 2012, due to Mayan predictions or anything else.   He is perhaps the only individual who could, through Executive Orders, create positive actions quickly. He alone is best positioned from the "bully pulpit" to issue assurances that the government has done everything possible to protect us from the unthinkable and assure our survival as a nation.

Next on the list logically would be Vice President Biden. Perhaps he could leave some legacy beyond his many speaking gaffes!   As mentioned earlier, Hillary Clinton actually has experience in a similar potential-disaster situation. Because of her experience with the Millennium Project guiding us through the remediation of the Y2K apocalypse scenario, she could take a major leadership role in public awareness and preparedness for any 2012 catastrophes.

You should write to Michelle Obama. She seems to be an empathic individual, and perhaps not as consumed time-wise as is her husband. Many would listen to her advice.

Perhaps logically the best person to write is Republican presidential candidate Mitt Romney. He could score huge political points on the "awareness" angle. He could talk pointedly about cyber-warfare and steps he would take to protect us. He could talk about the very real problem of solar mass ejections. He could talk about the dangers of nuclear war and what can be done to keep the largest number of Americans alive. He could explain what we are doing to negate cyber-attacks. Of course this assumes he and those around him have a clue, which is far from certainty.

Romney could at least mention December 21st. He could be the "Protector of the People!", a mantle that no one else seems to choose to wear at this time.   We certainly need someone to step up to the plate. Perhaps he could be that person. He certainly isn't going to become the next President emulating John McCain's "nice guy" strategy. Nice guys always finish last. It's the way of the jungle.

Your two Senators and your Representative in the House must be made aware of your concerns. I suspect there may actually be un-reported Congressional committees addressing some of these issues, but is anything being done for your immediate area? Write to your State Governor, who has the power to call out the National Guard in an emergency. He or she can also make directives to statewide groups to begin to make contingency plans for your survival. Government needs a wake-up call!

There are also local County officials to whom you could write, as well as your Mayor if you have one. The closer the mail recipient is to your home the more relevant any actions taken might be to you and yours. Do not forget to write to your local police, fire district and sheriff. They must grasp the seriousness of the situation and stand ready to help in a 2012 crisis which they may not yet perceive as a real viable threat.

Your special Holy-Person, be it a pastor, priest, rabbi, minister, Imam, guru or whichever, must be made aware of the dangers we face. I have spoken to a few and get a blank stare. Very sad.

Lastly, your child's school principal AND teacher, or college Dean needs to understand the potential survival problems we face. Some may be clueless, and some may themselves be terrified. As we approach December 21st the kids are going to hear all sorts of very alarming things about "the end of the world". Some may be very frightened. How do they plan to respond to the inevitable questions?

I recall how I felt in the '40s when we had the scary "under the desk, face away from the windows" drills because the Germans or Japanese were going to target my Public School 139 in Brooklyn! In retrospect I believe they would have had other targets in mind.

Perhaps more important than all of the above would be your letters to various celebrities. Radio and TV talk-show hosts would be a good start. Try Rush Limbaugh, Bill Maher, Dr. Michael Savage, Sean Hannity, Glenn Beck, Jay Leno, David Letterman, or whoever you listen to or watch, irrespective of your political persuasion or theirs. Musicians such as the greats Bono and Bruce Springsteen would have a large following, as would Madonna and Lady GaGa.

Sports heroes such as Michael Jordan or Tiger Woods, Joe Montana or Alex Rodriguez, or Tim Tebow would also be great survival spokespersons. To reach the younger set, who better than Justin Bieber and Selena Gomez? We need to get the word out, and to get the government to begin a plan to keep America safe and as a viable nation in the face of real dangers.

What should you say in your letters? I am going to suggest, for consistency and simplicity, that your opening and closing paragraphs should be identical to (or at least closely similar to) those written below. Sandwiched between these opening and closing paragraphs will be "middle paragraphs" tailored to each specific individual.

Of course you can write whatever you want, but the general content and emphasis should be similar to these suggestions. Please consider having your friends and family, and your Facebook, Twitter or other social media followers, do the same. We are quickly running out of time.

SUGGESTED OPENING PARAGRAPHS FOR EACH LETTER

Dear (whichever person you are addressing);

I have just finished reading a new book: *Apocalypse 12-21-12 The Mayan Prophecies*, available on line and at

Amazon Books and eReaders. I have also read a large number of articles on the internet and in newspapers. Many of these suggest that we are in no imminent danger. Others clearly suggest that we are, and for a startlingly large variety of reasons. Frankly, I am (fill in your true feelings: terrified; scared to death; deeply troubled; seriously concerned; troubled; upset, disturbed) that there are imminent dangers that are not being explained to the American public and may even be purposely withheld from us for fear of panic.

I am equally concerned that no preparations whatsoever are being made to insure our survival as a nation of free individuals in the event of one of the following real possibilities: A solar storm cripples our electric grid for an extended time period; A cyber-attack cripples our electric grid for weeks, months or even years; A nuclear war, localized or worldwide, brings on the unthinkable. Might not some Islamic madman seize upon 12/21/12 to create a self-fulfilling doomsday prophecy? These are just a few of the disasters I believe are facing us in 2012.

(INSERT THE SPECIAL INDIVIDUALIZED PARAGRAPHS HERE, BETWEEN THE ABOVE OPENING AND BELOW CLOSING PARAGRAPHS)

SUGGESTED CLOSING PARAGRAPHS FOR EACH LETTER

Please, I urge you, respect the opinions expressed by many independent scientists and others who believe we are in very serious imminent danger. A recent very credible study was reported by Reuters showing that over 22% of adult Americans believe that some imminent disaster will in fact in some way result in the end of their life. Similar beliefs are held worldwide by tens of millions of individuals. This is not a joking matter.

Please do not dismiss the "doomsayers" out of hand. Do not heed the posturing of some politicians whose personal agendas could jeopardize public safety. This is an unprecedented scenario in human history. Cultures around the world, not only the Mayans, see 2012 as a turning point for civilization. Time for action is very short. It will require strong, focused, honest leadership. As citizens we expect no less than the whole truth from our government no matter how painful or difficult that truth may be to hear.

I look forward to your reply at your earliest convenience. Thank you very much for your attention to this letter.

Very truly yours,

(SIGNED)

SUGGESTED INDIVIDUAL MIDDLE PARAGRAPHS

SUGGESTED CONTENT FOR YOUR LETTER TO THE PRESIDENT

I have listened intently to your many speeches, including the State of the Union speech, and have heard nothing from you regarding the implications of the very serious dangers we face in 2012, and potentially on December 21st. This would seem to imply that you do not believe that it is a matter of grave national importance. (NOTE: Omit this paragraph if such a speech has been made by the President by the time you read this).

What assurances can you offer my family and me that we do not need to prepare for a long time period without electric power or telephones? Without any possible means of mass transportation, can you assure us we will have water, and food, and heat throughout 2012 and beyond. At what point of the inevitable massive civil unrest would you declare Martial Law?

Would our personal weapons and ammunition be confiscated? Are there any plans for 100% transformer redundancy at our power plants? Are there any plans for massive water and food storage centers throughout the country? What do you suggest we do to prepare ourselves and our loved ones?

SUGGESTED CONTENT FOR YOUR LETTER TO MICHELLE OBAMA

I am very impressed with your efforts to instill a sense of physical fitness in our youth. You are obviously someone who many respect and to whom many listen. In that context, could you please become involved in creating an awareness of the potential life-threatening events that could occur later in 2012. In 1999 President Clinton put his wife in charge of the Millennium Project, an effort to create awareness and urgency over a potentially devastating event known as Y2K. The December 21, 2012 Mayan Calendar matter is at least as important today as Y2K was then, probably even more so.

Many Americans are very frightened. Many believe we are not being told the truth. Many believe the government is intentionally keeping the facts from us for fear of panic. Others fear even more that the government is both clueless and powerless to actually do anything to help us survive as a Nation. President Obama, were he to seize the initiative on this matter, and address it directly, could assure his re-election.

SUGGESTED CONTENT FOR YOUR LETTER TO THE VICE PRESIDENT

I have heard nothing from you or the President regarding the seriousness of these matters. There are a few questions to which I would appreciate answers.   If food becomes unavailable because all transportation is halted, does the government have plans in place to set up thousands of local water and food depots to insure our survival? Are there plans in place to deal with the inevitable widespread civil disobedience?   How do you propose to keep northerners from freezing to death? What suggestions do you have for me to protect my family?

SUGGESTED CONTENT FOR YOUR LETTER TO HILLARY CLINTON

During your husband's State of the Union speech some years ago he acknowledged your work as head of the Millennium Project, and you received a standing ovation. We face today a situation not unlike Y2K, though we cannot spend ourselves out of this one. I would appreciate it if you would respond to a few questions that are troubling me.

How should I and my family prepare for the above mentioned disaster scenarios in 2012 and beyond? What do you see our government doing for American citizens should one or more of these likely scenarios happen in 2012? Are you or anyone you know of in government taking this entire matter seriously? Will we have access to food and water when the electric grid collapses? In the face of the inevitable massive civil disobedience, at what point to you believe the President will invoke Executive Orders suspending all our civil liberties?

SUGGESTED CONTENT FOR YOUR LETTER TO MITT ROMNEY

You are in a position to make a stark contrast between yourself and our present government officials. I believe that the possible 2012 scenarios and their implications far outweigh any problems with the economy, unemployment, debt crisis, or health care. We are talking here about survival as a society, which is gravely threatened. Are you aware of the above mentioned imminent problems? Do you have any suggestions as to how the government, whose primary job is to protect its citizens, could save our society with positive actions?

You alone could seize the initiative on this matter, even simply by acknowledging your awareness of what many already believe to be inevitable. Positive statements such as suggesting policies mandating immediate 100% transformer redundancy at our power plants, and establishing massive water and food storage depots, would go a long way towards reducing public fears and insuring confidence in your leadership potential. I believe it would insure your election.

SUGGESTED CONTENT FOR YOUR LETTERS TO YOUR UNITED STATES SENATORS & REPRESENTATIVE, AND YOUR GOVERNOR

If there are any discussions about various 2012 disaster scenarios going on at the committee level these have not been reported in the media. As one of your constituents I have a number of questions that have been troubling my neighbors and me. What is the government doing to insure we have a viable electric grid in the event of 100% collapse due to a cyber-attack or a massive solar flare? What is being done to assure that we have country-wide local depots containing water and food for a year or more?

What contingency plans are in place for massive civil disobedience in a major crisis? Can we be assured that a well-fed Army or National Guard will protect us? How is the government planning to protect us in the event of a nuclear exchange? Are you taking the 2012 apocalyptic predictions seriously as are millions worldwide?

SUGGESTED CONTENT FOR YOUR LETTERS TO LOCAL POLITICIANS, YOUR SHERIFF, POLICE CHIEF AND FIRE OFFICIALS

I have seen nothing in the media from you about any of the above concerns. Are you aware of this 2012 apocalypse matter and taking it seriously? What local contingency plans are there to hydrate and feed citizens in the event obtaining water and food is impossible for a very long time? What about heat in the winter? Will there be any mass shelters available? Are plans in place for containing the inevitable wide-spread civil disobedience? With 911 services out, how do you suggest we communicate our urgent needs? What do you suggest we can do now to protect ourselves and our loved ones? What help do you expect from Washington? Are you considering establishing solar-powered short-wave communication capabilities?

SUGGESTED CONTENT FOR YOUR LETTER TO YOUR PERSONAL HOLY-PERSON

What part does God play in this frightening scenario? Are you sufficiently aware of all of the implications of the December 21st date? Your followers will be asking you many questions in the months and weeks before December 21st. Are you prepared to answer them? Are you planning any special sermons or messages to address this matter? Can I rely on my church to provide shelter and sustenance when the power grid goes down for a long period of time? Have you considered setting up a solar-powered short-wave communication system? What preparations do you believe I should be making for my family's survival at this special time? I do not believe prayer alone is sufficient.

SUGGESTED CONTENT FOR YOUR LETTER TO EDUCATORS

Are you sufficiently aware of the entire 2012 scenario to be able to properly counsel students under your care? They will be hearing many very many frightening things in the months and weeks leading up to December 21st. They will be hearing some lies, and some half-truths, and some painful real truths. How do you plan to respond to their questions? Will you be able to offer them any assurance that their government is taking every possible step to protect them? Will you try to minimize their anxiety, or will you provide them with straightforward, honest assessments of this frightening situation.

SUGGESTED CONTENT FOR YOUR LETTER TO CELEBRITIES

As a famous and respected celebrity you are in a unique position to speak to the public about the dangers we face in 2012, and especially December 21st. Have you taken the time to study the very real dangers we face and the gross lack of preparedness on the part of most Americans? Has the government let us down by not making our survival as a society as important as bickering over health care, the economy and the national debt?

That's it for the letter suggestions. A few persons to whom I have spoken are reluctant to write to government officials. Remember, we have a Constitutional Federal Government, "By the people, For the people". Whether it will perish from this earth is largely in the hands of the politicians. You MUST make them and others aware of your concerns.

You are certainly entitled to answers to your letters. Please do not hesitate to write. You can find specific addresses for politicians and celebrities easily with a Google search. Please do not wait for responses to your letters before taking serious preparedness steps.

At the very least, by writing these letters you will be increasing awareness among key individuals and doing your part in potentially having a positive effect on millions of lives. If some of these powerful individuals get enough letters from concerned citizens such as you perhaps they will initiate some positive action. Hope springs eternal.

I cannot say whether there is widespread ignorance, widespread apathy, a sense of denial, or a general conspiracy of silence. I can say that at this writing I see nothing comforting coming from any level of government, nor even an acknowledgment that they are looking into the critical problems we face on any level.

Are solutions being proposed by the government that have not yet been revealed to the public? I do see a lot of very credible scientists warning us in various obscure press releases and seldom-read scientific journals about the real dangers we face, and whether or not there is any validity to the December 21st doomsday predictions. Yet the general press is totally silent. I see nothing whatsoever out of Washington on any level. I only hope someone important is listening, and actually doing something. Time is getting very short.

PART TEN

<u>CONCLUSIONS</u>

"God, what fools these mortals be."
William Shakespeare, *A Midsummer
Night's Dream*.

"I can't think about that right now. If I
do, I'll go crazy. I'll think about that
tomorrow." Scarlett O'Hara, *Gone With
The Wind*.

"I never think of the future. It comes
soon enough." Albert Einstein.

PLEASE STOP!!! If you have not read
every page of this book please don't
start here. I know it's human nature,
but it is self-defeating to read the end of
this book first. It is not my intention to
give you MY conclusions. It is YOUR
conclusions that matter. The important
thing is for you to form your own
opinions and conclusions **after** reading
everything I share with you in the pages

that precede this "Part Ten - Conclusions" chapter.

You may read this book and come away with the conclusion that this entire "Mayan Apocalypse" matter is much ado about nothing. Then again, you might come to the opposite conclusion and make preparations for varying degrees of catastrophe. In either event, you should have enough information from the pages of this book to form a considered opinion, which was my objective in writing it.

My eyes glaze over reading all of the conflicting theories as to why the world as we know it will end this year. It could be the end of the Fourth World (per Maya and Hopi), or the end of the Fifth World (Aztec). It may be the Maori "Fall of the Curtain" or "Dissolving of the Void", when sky and earth meet, whatever the heck that means.

Mathematical proofs aside, there is a bewildering amount of conjecture regarding celestial alignments and their significance to the December 21st date. Relationships with the Pleiades asterism and in particular one of its stars, Alcione, abound. The constellation Orion enters the picture often. So does the Milky Way Galaxy, and the dark lanes between the spiral arms, as well as alignment with the Galactic Center itself.

Toss in various relationships with the planet Venus, Crop Circles, and Auric Time Scales and you end up with a hodgepodge of metaphysical gibberish that is absolutely impossible to reconcile. The problem is, someone just might be right. The big question is: "Who just might be spot on?".

My brain gets numb when I read, under a sub-chapter: "Gnostic Soulcraft", that: "The alignment with the solstice Sun with the galactic equator, close to Galactic Center at the start of Sagittarius, is thus a time when the galactic pineal eye will radiate its light and restore our individual pineal eyes to their full potential of transmundane vision." Seriously? Damn! I never even thought of **that** possibility! Perhaps my dog did.

This is a tiny out-of-context quote from Geof Stray's "*Beyond 2012 – Catastrophe or Awakening?*", copyright 2005, Bear & Company. Get the picture? Some of the stuff written on 2012's possible events is a bit hard to comprehend!

Actually, the above obscure passage aside, of all of the books listed in my Bibliography, Stray's 493 page tome is the most complete in outlining the many diverse cross-cultural 2012 theories. It is a very interesting read. There is a common thread throughout almost all of the books listed below that 2012 is a very special year for humans. Few of the books agree on what, why and how. Many of the books are rather confusing.

But one fact is amazingly clear: the year 2012 is deeply ingrained in many diverse cultures across the globe as a **critical end point** in human evolution. Cultures with no possible physical connection or means to have cross-pollinated ideas have come to this same conclusion. The year 2012 is **IT**.

It is this fact, and this fact alone, that has to make one at least take notice of the possibility that 2012 is very special and that they might all just happen to be right!

It has been reported that a gentleman in Romania had a divine vision twenty years ago that 2012 would be the end of the world. He was so totally convinced of this that years ago he purchased his gravesite and commissioned a cross inscribed with his impending 2012 date of death. Talk about a pessimist!

Let's look at all of this from a different perspective. Let's assume for the moment that the Mayan Calendar is absolutely meaningless. Let's accept that it simply ends one calendar cycle and another calendar picks up and the whole cycle just starts over. This is exactly the same as you and I discarding the 2012 calendar for the 2013 version on December 31st.

But that very Mayan calendar is not the only thing "carved in stone". THE VERY DATE, December 21, 2012 itself is, in a sense, carved in stone in our minds. It has been for many years. Were it not so ingrained in our consciousness over the past decades so many people worldwide would not be so very worried.

Something very unusual does seem to be afoot. Increased frequency and intensity of earthquakes, volcanos, and bizarre weather may well portend something much worse. We have the coming peak of the sun's activity cycle of activity to worry about.

But there has been one relatively recent social change beyond anything ever seen in the history of man. No, I'm not talking about the internet or Facebook or Twitter or Pinterest or YouTube.

I'm speaking about well-educated young men and women of average or better means that are willing to blow themselves up amidst members of their own religion, even those at prayer, weddings and funerals, for "the cause". Is this bizarre behavior the oft-forecast "prelude to the Apocalypse"?

We have heard about December 21, 2012 as "doomsday" for so long it resides deep within our consciousness. It is for this reason alone, a "special" date when either something big, or nothing at all of note will occur, that makes the date suspect.

Could we have created a self-fulfilling prophesy? We expect "something", even if that something ends up to be nothing! If some madman or terrorist group is planning a catastrophic event, what a perfect day to make it happen!

What is of very great concern is how millions worldwide today rely on "social networks" for information. You have surely heard about the radio broadcast decades ago of H. G. Wells classic "*War Of The Worlds*". It was so believable that thousands listening on their radios in poured out into the streets in total panic!

Recently an incident in China showed how this same scenario could play out today, not because of a radio or TV show, but because of the social network. Back in April rumors of a possible coup circulated widely throughout China's social networks. There were "eye-witness reports" of gunshots, and of tanks roaring through the streets of Beijing. None of this was happening. It was a complete and utter fabrication, but it caused widespread panic throughout the country.

What if such false information was put out by someone in high authority, or someone posing as such, here in the USA, some time around December 21st? Tens of millions would read it almost immediately, and depending on the message it would very likely cause widespread panic.

Widespread panic and civil disobedience does not seem too far fetched in our society today. How much can our citizens endure before they have had enough? What could be the all-out civil-disobedience tipping point? Or has our pathetic progressive public-education system so dumbed us down that we don't even HAVE a tipping point?

For examples, could our citizens finally learning all of the details of all of the clauses in the "Health Care Bill" that have absolutely nothing to do with health care itself lead to riots? Such as what clauses, you ask? How about the 3.8% tax on real estate profits to take effect 01/01/13? That's a Dusie! How about the dozen-plus other tax hikes buried in the bill? Now that our Supreme Court has given a thumbs-up to the bill these taxes and many other new taxes will be needed to pay for it.

Or how about the new ability that the government will have to make unauthorized electronic withdrawals from your bank account? Has anyone, including our elected representatives, actually READ that monstrosity of a bill in its entirety? Ms. Pelosi was so right when she said we'll all just have to read the bill after it passes to know what's in it. Of course, few bothered to make the effort.

We are lied to month in and month out. Why should we believe anything the government tells us about December 21st?

Need real examples? Take unemployment figures. For the past fifty or so weeks almost every Thursday's figure is made to look positive by revising the previous Thursday's figure however needed to make it look positive! Fuzzy math at its most insidious. We are truly the laughing stock of the planet. Very sad.

Not unlike the fuzzy math behind the employment figures, in reality our unemployment figure is more like twenty percent than the reported eight percent. It's just a matter of conveniently not counting those who have simply quit looking for work. More fuzzy math.

Or take the very low reported inflation numbers. If some item in the "market basket" used for that calculation would inconveniently cause the inflation number to be higher than some "desired target" number, simply "fuzzy-math" that item right out of the market basket. Presto! As if by magic, we have lower reported inflation. Time to rejoice? I think not. Truth? December 21st? We shall see.

Is that mushroom national symbol looking any better?

How is this for one hell of a coincidence? The numeric calendar date on the day before "doomsday"

December 21, 2012 is: 20.12.2012! (in year/day/month format). For the curious, this calendar oddity cannot happen again for another 189+ years, on January 30, 3001 (30.01.3001). Omen? Meaningless? Certainly interesting at the very least. I truly HATE coincidences. 2012 Kablooie? We shall see.

Let's take a brief look at the MENSANS, the high IQ society folk, supposedly among the smartest persons on the planet. They number the late great sci-fi author Isaac Asimov among their more famous past members, along with Jerry Seinfeld, Greta Van Susteren, Sonny Bono and John Travolta. (Incidentally, with 140 million potential earthling members, it isn't as exclusive a group as many MENSANS would like you to believe!)

These "brilliant" folk just held a highly-publicized event they bill as "The End Of

Time Activity Group" mega-party in Reno, Nevada July 4th through 8th. I'm assuming it was a lighthearted "jokeathon", but you never know. They had thousands of attendees. The media will doubtless report on this gathering as "a bunch of conspiracy-theory eggheads predicting the end of life as we know it". They might be right.

I am told I am one of the remaining 140 or so original American Mensans still alive today, having joined back in the '60s when they first came to America from Britain. I figure I'll have to live another twenty or so years to be the single oldest living American Mensan (I'm 75 now.) Damn it, shouldn't everyone have a goal? (PS: I did not attend The End of Time MENSA event in Reno. I'm be too busy preparing for 12/21!)

Though early July seems a bit premature to have a "kiss your ass goodbye" party, I'm sure as 12/21 approaches there will be many more such parties of all sizes across the globe. Some will be held as a joke, an occasion to get drunk and have fun. Some will be deadly serious gatherings of people who truly believe their lives are about to end and are scared stiff. There may even be many suicides related to the fast-approaching date.

Late-night comics like Leno and Letterman, and every cartoonist on earth, will have more joke material over this "Apocalypse" than they can ever use! I can't wait to see Letterman's "Ten Best Reasons Why We're All Going To Die On December 21st".

As I pointed out earlier, polls indicate that there are many millions of people who deeply believe in the coming Apocalypse.   The more the government (which isn't exactly high on most people's trust-list) assures us that the whole thing is a hoax the more who will become believers in Doomsday!

Election day is only seven or so weeks before the Mayan long-count calendar expires. Beyond a doubt, probably in late summer, questions about "doomsday" will be coming in from all over the world. Tens of thousands of questions. At some point before the election I believe both presidential candidates will be forced to make some serious statements about December 21st.

Will either candidate actually level with the American public and outline the very real risks we face, before, on, or soon after December 21st, and advise us all to make life-saving preparations? Does either candidate have the will to honestly tell Americans something they would surely rather not hear? Ignorance is bliss?

For whom would you vote? The candidate that almost inevitably will make a joke out of it? This is the candidate who will continue to minimize the dangers, quoting all manner of NASA experts as proof-positive that the whole matter is meaningless.

Or would you vote for a candidate who candidly acknowledges that we are at very high risk, be it from a nuclear-armed Iran, an impending cyber-attack, a solar flare, a space rock, or any of a number of other remote-to-possible scenarios? Would said candidate dare tell the public that we should be prepared for life-without-electricity for some unknown period of time?

What about a candidate who pledges to insist on power plant transformer 100% redundancy, and to establishing thousands of food and potable water storage facilities throughout the country? Would either candidate ever even remotely consider mentioning such a critical matter? Sadly, I doubt it. We'll see.

Here's an interesting thought. If there is mass panic before November 6th, which is not beyond possibility, could a National Emergency be declared and the Presidential elections be postponed indefinitely? Just a thought.

We're far too obsessed with concerns about gay marriage, and who pays for contraceptives, and who was born where, or whose religion is a cult, than we are in preserving the Nation in the event of some catastrophe for which we are utterly and quite needlessly unprepared. We **must** prepare.

Y2K was not a hoax, though the government at the time would have had you believe there was zero danger. That was a big lie. The trillions of dollars spent to prevent that "hoax" from happening speaks volumes. We dodged a bullet because we could buy our way out of a real serious danger. Will we dodge this one? You simply cannot buy your way out of any of the many possible doomsday scenarios. You can only prepare to survive.

There will be a very interesting period of forty-four days between the presidential election on November 6th and the Mayan "End Of Time" December 21st. Win or lose, Barack Obama will be President, either as a lame duck, or headed for a second term.

This time period will coincide with massive worldwide public interest in "Doomsday". It could even lead to mass hysteria and riots, depending on how the media and governments worldwide handle presenting information to the masses.

One need not look any further than the leftist-sponsored anarchist "Occupy" movement to see how ugly a hate-filled mob with no definable agenda other than "change" can get. Multiply that by thousands of panicky, really frightened people, in every major city in the world, and we could have an Apocalypse of sorts even if absolutely nothing at all actually comes to pass.

Would this not be a logical time to declare a "National Emergency" and institute martial law? As good a time as any. I find that scenario at least as frightening as being zapped by aliens! But what is even scarier is that, if one can imagine a madman starting WWIII on 12/21 as an ironic joke (again, as good a day as any) martial law might not be all that bad an idea. We're I President I would surely consider it. We shall see.

If the Mayan Calendar matter doesn't scare the hell out of you, perhaps this will: Don Miller, Contributing Writer, Monday Morning, dateline June 6, 2012 wrote: "Are You Ready for "Taxmageddon"? A slow moving train wreck known as Taxmageddon is creeping towards U. S. taxpayers. You see, if Congress doesn't act by year's end, numerous tax breaks will expire.... and hit every American squarely in the wallet. It's a fiscal tsunami that will strike as early as December. The damage will be so widespread it could derail the entire U. S. economy. Nobody in Washington, however, is doing anything about it."

And this does not include all of the added taxes in the Affordable Health Care Act. This could be a really interesting December! Combine Taxmageddon with Armageddon: 2012 Kablooie?

Personally I still grieve over the death of astronomer Carl Sagan. His video series: "COSMOS" was one of the most eye-opening discourses on science ever created. Invoking his famous maxim, he said: "Extraordinary claims require extraordinary evidence. Since the beginning of time there have been literally hundreds of thousands of predictions for the end of the world, and we're still here." He failed to add: "…at least until 12/21/12"!

Think of the life of earth as a 12 month 365 day calendar. Man-like mammals first appear somewhere after mid-December! The 236 year old USA appears in the last few moments of the year! So the contention that "we are still here" after all prior doomsday predictions failed to pan out is rather weak in light of the very little time we've actually BEEN here!

IF this coming December date could actually have some validity, and dire predictions become reality, should not the various religious institutions worldwide soon begin warning their flocks? Should not governments everywhere be setting up contingency plans and stocking food-dispersal sites? This was actually done by some American cities prior to the Y2K "non-event".

In the event of the unthinkable, human civilization can only survive through extensive mutual cooperation. If chaos ensues, and law and order breaks down, Hollywood's most pessimistic post-apocalypse worlds will seem as paradise! Remember: *"Hunger Games"; The Postman"; "Water World"; "I Am Legend"?*

Can you imagine yourself living in a post-apocalyptic world? I cannot. Yet we all may be forced to, like it or not.

We've only been here as a sentient species for a very short time in terms of the age of the earth or the universe. Somewhere along the line one of these Apocalypse predictions, by divine design or pure accident, logically figures to come true. Will you be ready?

Next week, or on December 21st, or on some date in the future, we are surely all, at the very least, "light toast". Preparing for a "worst case scenario", thoroughly burnt toast, or just a "very bad case scenario", is a really good idea.

Please, please take the information in this book seriously. Take action now. Don't wait. Don't procrastinate. There may be very little time. You cannot wait until early December to begin your preparations.

Many preparations are inexpensive, especially weighed against the awful possible consequences of inaction. Bite the bullet. Do whatever you possibly can for the sake of your loved ones. Some preparation is better than no preparation. Do it now!

REMEMBER: NO ONE IS PROMISED TOMORROW.

GOD bless you all.

Live long and prosper.

GOD BLESS AMERICA. (And be on the lookout for that great "Apocalypse" campaign speech!)

Happy December 22nd!

ABOUT THE AUTHOR

"I am what I am." Popeye.

James Burton Anderson is an engineering graduate of the Polytechnic Institute (now NYU – Poly), holds a Master's degree from CCNY, and is a life-long "astronomy-nut".

Some twenty years ago Burt became deeply interested in both the Y2K scenario and in the Mayan "End Of Time" calendar issues. He has studied Mayan Calendar matters extensively and read and analyzed almost all of the available literature on the subject, which is considerable.

Because of this, and his life-long interest in astronomy, plus his exceptional scientific background, Burt has forged valuable insights about 12/21/12 that are seldom discussed or revealed anywhere else. He shares his unique perspective on what could occur both before, on, and after December 21, 2012.

Both of his academic degrees were earned in night school while he worked daytime jobs to pay for all of his tuition. No loans, no scholarships, just nine years of long hours and hard work and little sleep.

As a teenager, Burt became one of the first one-thousand members of American MENSA, the high IQ society, in which he has been quite active. He is one of the last surviving 133 members of that early era in MENSA history. He believes that his God-given intelligence allows him to see and analyze complex matters such as the Mayan Calendars' meanings and break them down into bite-sized easy-to-understand pieces.

He's in now in his 75th year of life, which he says qualifies him as an "official old fart"!   A very prolific author since 1970, he has been directly involved in internet communication since 1996, which also qualifies him as "very old" in terms of the age of the internet. He believes that this internet knowledge puts him in a unique position to "get the truth out" about the coming "End of Time", the so-called "Mayan Calendar Prophecies".

He is responsible for eleven books and countless articles. His optimistic "Whitewash Y2K" was one of the many popular books addressing the "millennium bug". He has been published in "*Leaders*" magazine, which is sent only to country heads-of-state and business CEOs.

He considers the remoteness of his home and the high degree of preparedness he has created for his family, to be optimal for enduring many of the potential "doomsday" scenarios, should they actually come to pass. Burt says: "And they WILL come to pass, if not on precisely 12/21/12 then eventually in my lifetime."

He is a proud American Legion member, and volunteers his time freely to various local non-profit groups. Married with four children and two grandchildren, he lives with his wife of thirty years and two great pups in Arizona's High Sonoran Desert.

Burt insists that: "Knowledge is power. If I can help others understand what possible scenarios we may face as December 21st approaches, great! If what I offer eases some folk's anxiety, that's also great. If it scares some others into action, that's even better!" Only time will tell.

BIBLIOGRAPHY

"The more you read the more things you will know." Theodore Geisel .... Dr. Seuss.

Here is a short sample, listed alphabetically, of some of the 2012 "End of Time" related books in my personal library, which contains an eclectic mix of over 10,000 volumes. I have read each of the 2012s at least twice, most when they were first published, and again within the past year. For the most part their theme is consistent.

The year 2012 is the big year for something earth-changing to happen. Their conclusions relating to what may happen, what will cause it to happen, and on what date, differ greatly.

Some of these books have been re-copyrighted in 2011 and 2012 for Amazon and Google electronic delivery.

Interestingly, in most not a single word of text has been changed! It seems that theories postulated ten or more years ago are just as valid today as they were then. Or perhaps the authors are simple too lazy to re-write them!

Some authors focus on the rare alignment of various stars and planets. Others focus on the effect on earth of a major solar flare, which some postulate will flip earth's poles with cataclysmic effects. Others focus on religion. Some offer extremely detailed arithmetic calculations as irrefutable proof of the coming Apocalypse.

Some authors even claim a Mayan connection with Atlantis! What I find most intriguing is that almost all speak of a "beginning time" and an "end time", and the general focus, as it has been for a half-century or more, has been on the year 2012 as being that end time year.

There will be dozens of new books published on the subject of the "End of Time", the Apocalypse, with various predictions by many authors to be published or re-published this year. Many of these older books were written in German and have never been translated into English.

An internet search will turn up more books and articles than one could possibly read before December 21st. After that, reading them will either be totally academic, or a bit too late! Enjoy.

2012: A Clarion Call   Nicolya Christi   2011

2012 and the Galactic Center C. Page   2008

2012 and the Shift Of Ages   Alexander Price 2009

2012 – Mayan Year Of Destiny   Adrian Gilbert 2006

A Hitchhiker's Guide To Armageddon D. Childress   2001

Atlantis & 2012   Frank Joseph   2010

Beyond 2012 – Catastrophe or Awakening? Geof Stray   2005

Boca's Brain   Carl Sagan   1974

Breaking The Maya Code   Michael Coe   1994

Chariots Of The Gods   Erich von Daniken   1969

Cosmos   Carl Sagan   1980

Galactic Alignment   John Jenkins   2002

Hall of the Gods Nigel Appelby   1998

How To Survive 2012   Patrick Geryl   2007

Maya Cosmogenesis 2012   John Jenkins   1998

Maya Cosmos   David Friedel et al   1993

Mexico Mystique   Frank Waters   1975

Mystery Of The Crystal Skulls   Morton & Thomas   2002

Reading The Maya Glyphs   Michael Coe   2001

Return Of The Serpents Of Wisdom M.Pinkham   1998

Shift of the Ages   David Wilcock   2000

Signs In The Sky   Adrian Gilbert   2001

Technology Of The Gods   David Childress   2000

The Canopus Revelation   Philip Coppens   2004

The Maya   Michael Coe   1966, 1993

The Maya Book Of The Dead   F. Robicsek   1981

The Mayan Calendar   John Calleman   2004

The Mayan Code   Barbara Clow   2007

The Mayan Factor   Jose Arguelles   1987

The Mayan Prophesies   M.Cotterell & A.Gilbert 1995

The Orion Mystery R. Bauval & Adrian Gilbert 1995

The Orion Prophecy   Patrick Geryl   2002

The World Cataclysn In 2012 – Maya Countdown Patrick Geryl   2005

Time of the Quickening   Susan Martinez   2011

Twilight Of The Gods   Erich von Daniken   2010

Worlds In Collision   Immanuel Velikovsky   1971

APPENDIX – PREPAREDNESS RESOURCES

"The greatest antidote to worry, whether you're getting ready for space-flight or facing a problem of daily life, is preparation. The more you try to envision what might happen and what your best response and options are, the more you are able to allay your fears." Senior Astronaut John Glenn.

The list of websites that follows is very far from complete. All sites are active as of this writing. These are resources with which I have either dealt directly or know someone who has recommended them. Neither the author nor publisher receives compensation from any of these vendors for inclusion in this list. It is strongly suggested that you conduct your own Google search in each category.

Many items can be purchased from major retailers such as Home Depot, Lowes, Walmart, Target, LLBean, Buy.com, Amazon and eBay.

If you do not believe that survival preparedness is a very real and pressing issue, please take note of the many hundreds of companies that make a very good living offering these diverse products to a deeply concerned citizenry. If you choose to ignore making preparations for an inevitable emergency you will very likely be in a very small minority by mid-December 2012.

The following sites are listed in no particular order:

HOME SOLAR PANEL ELECTRIC SYSTEMS

www.wholesalesolar.com

www.mrsolar.com

www.sungevity.com

www.solarworld-usa.com

www.hometurnedgreen.com

WIND-DRIVEN HOME ELECTRIC GENERATORS

www.bergey.com

www.windenergy7.com

www.allsmallwindturbines.com

www.windustry.org

GASOLINE, DIESEL & PROPANE POWERED PORTABLE ELECTRIC GENERATORS

www.alten-dc.com

www.electricgenerators.com/diesel

www.generatordepot.us

www.duropower.com

SOLAR POWERED PORTABLE ELECTRIC GENERATORS

www.mysolarbackup.com

www.thousandsuns.com

www.earthteckproducts.com/generators

FREEZE DRIED MEALS FOR LONG-TERM STORAGE

www.nitro-pak.com

www.wisefoodstorage.com

www.freezedriedfood.com

www.survival-warehouse.com

www.myfoodstorage.com

www.freelegacyfood.com

SOLAR POWERED AM/FM RADIOS

www.quakekare.com

www.llbean.com/weather

www.ambientweather.com

SOLAR BATTERY CHARGERS

www.greenlivingeveryday.com

www.batteriesplus.com

www.rei.com/solar-chargers

www.store.sundancesolar.com/solbatch ar.html

SHORT WAVE RADIO ("HAM" RADIO)

www.universal-radio.com

www.hemisphere.com

www.hfradio.org

www.radiosurvivalist.com

WATER PURIFICATION

www.katadyn.com

www.noahwater.com

www.generalecology.com/category/port able

www.pleasanthillgrain.com

WATER STORAGE TANKS

www.ntotank.com

www.usplastics.com

www.tank-depot.com

www.plastic-mart.com/plasticwatertanks

Smithsonian magazine, June 2012: "The cold war is over, but the bomb shelter market is heating up, offering accommodations that will help you survive Armageddon in style."

FALLOUT SHELTERS

www.atlassurvivalshelters.com

www.bomb-shelter.net

www.2012shelters.net

www.risingscompany.com

www.undergroundbombshelter.com

SURVIVAL SKILLS

www.homelandsecurityequipment.com

www.wildwoodssurvival.com

www.wilderness-survival.net

FIRST AID AND MEDICINE

www.adventuremedicalkits.com

www.galls.com

www.firstaidstore.com

www.shelfreliance.com/emergencykits

www.first-aid-product.com

IODINE RADIATION TABLETS

www.nukepills.com

www.ki4u.com

www.campingsurvival.com/radiation

www.nutrasource.com/radiation_tablets

MISCELLANEOUS SURVIVAL GEAR

www.survivalcache.com

www.majorsurplus.com

www.survival-warehouse.com

www.1staidsupplies.com

www.preparedplanet.com

www.ahepherdsurvival.com

www.rothco.com/survival\supplies

PRECIOUS METALS

When it comes to buying precious metals, I have two strong recommendations.   Do not ever buy the various coins offered in magazine ads, and do not buy bullion or bullion coins from companies that advertise on TV. "One-percent over dealer cost" sounds great and may even be true, but it is meaningless to you in terms of getting the best possible price when you buy.

I see ads that offer coins for 25%-50% or more over the price for which a knowledgeable buyer can purchase the exact same coin or ounce of bouillon elsewhere.

Where is "elsewhere"? Go to www.coinworld.com. I suggest you buy one copy of their snail-mail weekly Coin World newspaper and keep it for reference. Most large libraries carry it as well. It contains hundreds of highly-competitive ads from very reputable companies. Most quote different prices in every issue because market values change constantly. All will adjust that price to follow the exact minute to minute true market prices during a phone-order call.

There are dozens of toll-free 800 numbers to call in order to compare prices. Before you call to buy bouillon or bullion coins check out www.kitco.com. You will find the literally up-to-the-minute precious metals prices so you can see exactly what premium you are paying to various vendors.

13439273R00168

Made in the USA
Charleston, SC
10 July 2012